IRISH
CHURCH PRAISE

An Authorized Supplement
to the 1960 Edition of the
Irish Church Hymnal

WORDS EDITION

ASSOCIATION FOR
PROMOTING CHRISTIAN KNOWLEDGE

OXFORD UNIVERSITY PRESS

1990

Jointly published by
Association for Promoting Christian Knowledge, Dublin
and

Oxford University Press, Walton Street, Oxford OX2 6DP

Oxford New York Toronto
Delhi Bombay Calcutta Madras Karachi
Petaling Jaya Singapore Hong Kong Tokyo
Nairobi Dar es Salaam Cape Town
Melbourne Auckland

and associated companies in
Berlin Ibadan

Oxford is a trade mark of Oxford University Press

For sale in the Republic of Ireland and Northern Ireland only

First printed in 1990
Reprinted in 1990 (twice)

ISBN 0 19 148151 3

Origination by Barnes Music Engraving Ltd.
Printed in Scotland

A Music Edition is also available

This collection of hymns was compiled by a committee set up by resolution of the General Synod of the Church of Ireland in 1987, following a suggestion from the Association for Promoting Christian Knowledge that the *Irish Church Hymnal* should be revised to meet the present needs of the Church. The Committee included nominees of the Standing Committee of the General Synod and of the APCK. The 1988 General Synod accepted the recommendation of the Committee that a broadly-based supplement to the *Irish Church Hymnal* should be compiled, submitted to the House of Bishops for approval, and published as soon as practicable, without prejudice to the later revision of the Hymnal.

CONTENTS

FOREWORD

by the Archbishop of Armagh and Primate of All Ireland,
The Most Reverend R. H. A. Eames

I have pleasure in commending this collection of hymns for use throughout the Church of Ireland. It is obvious that a great deal of thought and research has gone into its preparation, and I hope the book will be used regularly and widely in all our churches.

The Church of Ireland has a long and illustrious musical tradition. Many of our hymn-writers have found international acceptance and approval. The depth of spirituality, which has long been an integral part of our ethos, has been evident in the hymns used in parish churches throughout Ireland. But passing years have produced different attitudes to the ways in which we express our love for God in worship. This book takes account of such developments, and in it you will find hymns from a wide range of different sources. It is helpful to have some of the most popular of modern hymns included in one book. I am sure their use will add to the contemporary expression of the Faith we hold.

The House of Bishops welcomes the publication of this book and believes that clergy and parishioners alike will find in it much to enrich and renew their worship.

✠ ROBERT ARMAGH

1

Alleluia, alleluia, give thanks to the risen Lord!
Alleluia, alleluia, give praise to his name.

1 Jesus is Lord of all the earth.
   He is the King of creation.

2 Spread the good news through all the earth,
   Jesus has died and has risen:

3 We have been crucified with Christ—
   now we shall live for ever:

4 God has proclaimed the just reward—
   life for the world, alleluia!

5 Come, let us praise the living God,
   joyfully sing to our Saviour!

Donald Fishel (b. 1928)

2

1 Amazing grace (how sweet the sound!)
   that saved a wretch like me!
   I once was lost, but now am found;
   was blind, but now I see.

2 'Twas grace that taught my heart to fear,
   and grace my fears relieved;
   how precious did that grace appear
   the hour I first believed!

3 Through many dangers, toils and snares
   I have already come;
   'tis grace has brought me safe thus far,
   and grace will lead me home.

4 The Lord has promised good to me,
   his word my hope secures;
   he will my shield and portion be
   as long as life endures.

5 Yes, when this flesh and heart shall fail,
   and mortal life shall cease,
   I shall possess within the veil
   a life of joy and peace.

John Newton (1725–1807)

3

1 And can it be that I should gain
an interest in the Saviour's blood?
Died he for me, who caused his pain?
For me, who him to death pursued?
Amazing love! how can it be
that thou, my God, shouldst die for me! } *twice (etc.)*

2 He left his Father's throne above—
so free, so infinite his grace—
emptied himself of all but love,
and bled for Adam's helpless race.
'Tis mercy all, immense and free;
for, O my God, it found out me!

3 Long my imprisoned spirit lay
fast bound in sin and nature's night;
thine eye diffused a quickening ray—
I woke, the dungeon flamed with light;
my chains fell off, my heart was free.
I rose, went forth, and followed thee.

4 No condemnation now I dread;
Jesus, and all in him, is mine!
Alive in him, my living head,
and clothed in righteousness divine,
bold I approach the eternal throne,
and claim the crown, through Christ, my own.

Charles Wesley (1707–88)

4

A new commandment I give unto you,
that you love one another as I have loved you,
that you love one another as I have loved you.
By this shall all know that you are my disciples,
if you have love one to another.
By this shall all know that you are my disciples,
if you have love one to another.

John 13: 34–5

5

1 As the deer pants for the water,
   so my soul longs after you.
   You alone are my heart's desire
   and I long to worship you.

> *You alone are my strength, my shield,*
> *to you alone may my spirit yield.*
> *You alone are my heart's desire*
> *and I long to worship you.*

2 I want you more than gold or silver,
   only you can satisfy.
   You alone are the real joy-giver
   and the apple of my eye.

3 You're my friend and you are my brother,
   even though you are a king.
   I love you more than any other,
   so much more than anything.

Martin Nystrom

6

1 Awake, awake to love and work!
   The lark is in the sky,
   the fields are wet with diamond dew,
   the world's awake to cry
   their blessings on the Lord of life,
   as he goes meekly by.

2 Come, let thy voice be one with theirs,
   shout with their shout of praise;
   see how the giant sun soars up,
   great lord of years and days;
   so let the love of Jesus come,
   and set thy soul ablaze.

3 To give, and give, and give again,
   what God has given thee;
   to spend thyself, nor count the cost;
   to serve right gloriously
   the God who gave all worlds that are
   and all that are to be.

Geoffrey Anketell Studdert-Kennedy (1883–1929)

7

1 Be still, for the presence of the Lord, the Holy One is here.
Come, bow before him now, with reverence and fear.
In him no sin is found, we stand on holy ground.
Be still, for the presence of the Lord, the Holy One is here.

2 Be still, for the glory of the Lord is shining all around;
he burns with holy fire, with splendour he is crowned.
How awesome is the sight, our radiant King of light!
Be still, for the glory of the Lord is shining all around.

3 Be still, for the power of the Lord is moving in this place,
he comes to cleanse and heal, to minister his grace.
No work too hard for him, in faith receive from him;
be still, for the power of the Lord is moving in this place.

Dave Evans
based on Exodus 3: 1–6

8

1 Be still, my soul: the Lord is on thy side;
bear patiently the cross of grief or pain;
leave to thy God to order and provide;
in every change he faithful will remain.
Be still, my soul: thy best, thy heavenly friend
through thorny ways leads to a joyful end.

2 Be still, my soul: thy God doth undertake
to guide the future as he has the past.
Thy hope, thy confidence let nothing shake;
all now mysterious shall be bright at last.
Be still, my soul: the waves and winds still know
his voice who ruled them while he dwelt below.

3 Be still, my soul: when dearest friends depart,
and all is darkened in the vale of tears,
then shalt thou better know his love, his heart,
who comes to soothe thy sorrow and thy fears.
Be still, my soul: thy Jesus can repay,
from his own fullness, all he takes away.

4 Be still, my soul: the hour is hastening on
   when we shall be forever with the Lord,
   when disappointment, grief, and fear are gone,
   sorrow forgot, love's purest joys restored.
   Be still, my soul: when change and tears are past,
   all safe and blessèd we shall meet at last.

Katharina von Schlegel (1697–?)
tr. Jane Laurie Borthwick (1813–97)

9

1 Be strong in the Lord
   in armour of light!
   With helmet and sword,
   with shield for the fight;
   on prayer be dependent,
   be belted and shod,
   in breastplate resplendent—
   the armour of God.

2 Integrity gird
   you round to impart
   the truth of his word
   as truth in your heart:
   his righteousness wearing
   as breastplate of mail,
   his victory sharing,
   be strong to prevail.

3 With eagerness shod
   stand firm in your place,
   or go forth for God
   with news of his grace:
   no foe shall disarm you
   nor force you to yield,
   no arrow can harm you
   with faith as your shield.

4 Though Satan presume
   to test you and try,
   in helmet and plume
   your head shall be high:
   beset by temptation
   be true to your Lord,
   your helmet salvation
   and scripture your sword.

5 So wield well your blade,
   rejoice in its powers!
   Fight on undismayed
   for Jesus is ours!
   Then in him victorious
   your armour lay down,
   to praise, ever glorious,
   his cross and his crown.

Timothy Dudley-Smith (b. 1926)
based on Ephesians 6: 10–18

10

Bind us together, Lord,
bind us together
with cords that cannot be broken.
Bind us together, Lord,
bind us together,
O bind us together with love.

1 There is only one God.
   There is only one King.
   There is only one body;
   that is why we sing.

2 Made for the glory of God,
   purchased by his precious Son.
   Born with the right to be clean,
   for Jesus the victory has won.

3 You are the family of God.
   You are the promise divine.
   You are God's chosen desire.
   You are the glorious new wine.

Bob Gillman

11

1 Christ be beside me,
   Christ be before me,
   Christ be behind me,
   King of my heart.
   Christ be within me,
   Christ be below me,
   Christ be above me,
   never to part.

2 Christ on my right hand,
   Christ on my left hand,
   Christ all around me,
   shield in the strife.
   Christ in my sleeping,
   Christ in my sitting,
   Christ in my rising,
   light of my life.

3 Christ be in all hearts
   thinking about me,
   Christ be on all tongues
   telling of me.
   Christ be the vision
   in eyes that see me,
   in ears that hear me,
   Christ ever be.

James Quinn (b. 1919)
adapted from 'St Patrick's Breastplate'

12

1 Christ is alive! Let Christians sing;
   the cross stands empty to the sky;
   let streets and homes with praises ring;
   love drowned in death shall never die.

2 Christ is alive! No longer bound
   to distant years in Palestine;
   but saving, healing, here and now,
   and touching every place and time.

3 Not throned afar, remotely high,
   untouched, unmoved by human pains,
   but daily, in the midst of life,
   our Saviour in the Godhead reigns.

4 In every insult, rift and war,
   where colour, scorn or wealth divide,
   he suffers still, yet loves the more,
   and lives where even hope has died.

5 Christ is alive, and comes to bring
   new life to this and every age,
   till earth and all creation ring
   with joy, with justice, love, and praise.

Brian Arthur Wren (b. 1936)

13

1 Christ triumphant, ever reigning,
   Saviour, Master, King!
   Lord of heaven, our lives sustaining,
   hear us as we sing:

   Yours the glory and the crown,
   the high renown, th'eternal name!

2 Word incarnate, truth revealing,
   Son of Man on earth!
   Power and majesty concealing
   by your humble birth:

3 Suffering servant, scorned, ill-treated,
   victim crucified!
   Death is through the cross defeated,
   sinners justified:

4 Priestly king, enthroned for ever
   high in heaven above!
   Sin and death and hell shall never
   stifle hymns of love:

5 So, our hearts and voices raising
   through the ages long,
   ceaselessly upon you gazing,
   this shall be our song:

Michael John Saward (b. 1932)

14

1 Come to us, creative Spirit,
   in our Father's house;
   every human talent hallow,
   hidden skills arouse,
   that within your earthly temple,
   wise and simple
   may rejoice.

2 Poet, painter, music-maker
   all your treasures bring;
   craftsman, actor, graceful dancer
   make your offering;
   join your hands in celebration:
   let creation
   shout and sing!

3 Word from God eternal springing
   fill our minds, we pray;
   and in all artistic vision
   give integrity:
   may the flame within us burning
   kindle yearning
   day by day.

4 In all places and forever
   glory be expressed
   to the Son, with God the Father
   and the Spirit blessed:
   in our worship and our living
   keep us striving
   for the best.

David Mowbray (b. 1938)

15

1 Fairest Lord Jesus,
   Lord of all creation,
   Jesus, of God and Mary the Son;
   you will I cherish,
   you will I honour,
   you are my soul's delight and crown.

2 Fair are the meadows,
   fairer still the woodlands,
   robed in the verdure and bloom of spring.
   Jesus is fairer,
   Jesus is purer,
   he makes the saddest heart to sing.

3 Fair are the flowers,
  fairer still the children,
  in all the freshness of youth arrayed:
  yet is their beauty
  fading and fleeting;
  my Jesus, yours will never fade.

4 Fair is the sunshine,
  fairer still the moonlight
  and fair the twinkling starry host.
  Jesus shines brighter,
  Jesus shines clearer
  than all the stars that heaven can boast.

5 All fairest beauty.
  heavenly and earthly,
  wondrously, Jesus, in you I see;
  none can be nearer,
  fairer or dearer,
  than you, my Saviour, are to me.

from the German (Münster, 1677)
tr. Lilian Sinclair Stevenson (1870–1960)
and others

16

1 Father, Lord of all creation,
  ground of being, life and love;
  height and depth beyond description
  only life in you can prove:
  you are mortal life's dependence:
  thought, speech, sight are ours by grace;
  yours is every hour's existence,
  sovereign Lord of time and space.

2 Jesus Christ, the Man for others,
  we, your people, make our prayer:
  help us love—as sisters, brothers—
  all whose burdens we can share.
  Where your name binds us together
  you, Lord Christ, will surely be;
  where no selfishness can sever
  there your love the world may see.

3 Holy Spirit, rushing, burning
  wind and flame of Pentecost,
  fire our hearts afresh with yearning
  to regain what we have lost.
  May your love unite our action,
  nevermore to speak alone:
  God, in us abolish faction,
  God, through us your love make known.

Stewart Cross (1928–89)

17

1 Father, now behold us
  and this child, we pray:
  in your love enfold us,
  wash our sins away.

2 Christ's eternal blessing
  for this life we claim:
  faith, by ours, professing;
  signed in Jesus' Name.

3 By the Spirit tended
  childhood grow to youth,
  from all ill defended,
  full of grace and truth.

4 God of all creation,
  stoop from heaven's throne,
  and by Christ's salvation
  make this child your own.

Timothy Dudley-Smith (b. 1926)

18

1 Father, we adore you,
  lay our lives before you:
  how we love you!

2 Jesus, we adore you,
  lay our lives before you:
  how we love you!

3 Spirit, we adore you,
  lay our lives before you:
  how we love you!

Terrye Coelho

19

1 Father of mercy, God of consolation,
   look on your people, gathered here to praise you,
   pity our weakness, come in power to aid us,
   source of all blessing.

2 Son of the Father, Lord of all creation,
   come as our Saviour, Jesus, friend of sinners,
   grant us forgiveness, lift our downcast spirit,
   heal us and save us.

3 Life-giving Spirit, be our light in darkness,
   come to befriend us, help us bear our burdens,
   give us true courage, breathe your peace around us,
   stay with us always.

4 God in Three Persons, Father, Son and Spirit,
   come to renew us, fill your Church with glory,
   grant us your healing, pledge of resurrection,
   foretaste of heaven.

James Quinn (b. 1919)

20

1 Finished the strife of battle now,
   gloriously crowned the victor's brow:
   sing with gladness, hence with sadness:

   Alleluia, alleluia!

2 After the death that him befell,
   Jesus Christ has harrowed hell:
   songs of praising we are raising:

3 On the third morning he arose,
   shining with victory o'er his foes;
   earth is singing, heaven is ringing:

4 Lord, by your wounds on you we call:
   now that from death you've freed us all:
   may our living be thanksgiving:

Latin hymn, ? 17th cent.
tr. John Mason Neale (1818–66)

21

1 Forth in the peace of Christ we go;
  Christ to the world with joy we bring;
  Christ in our minds, Christ on our lips,
  Christ in our hearts, the world's true King.

2 King of our hearts, Christ makes us kings;
  kingship with him his servants gain;
  with Christ, the Servant-Lord of all,
  Christ's world we serve to share Christ's reign.

3 Priests of the world, Christ sends us forth
  this world of time to consecrate,
  our world of sin by grace to heal,
  Christ's world in Christ to re-create.

4 Prophets of Christ, we hear his word:
  he claims our minds, to search his ways,
  he claims our lips, to speak his truth,
  he claims our hearts, to sing his praise.

5 We are his Church, he makes us one:
  here is one hearth for all to find,
  here is one flock, one Shepherd-King,
  here is one faith, one heart, one mind.

James Quinn (b. 1919)

22

1 For the fruits of his creation,
  thanks be to God!
  For his gifts to every nation,
  thanks be to God!
  For the ploughing, sowing, reaping,
  silent growth while we are sleeping;
  future needs in earth's safe keeping,
  thanks be to God!

2 In the just reward of labour,
  God's will is done;
in the help we give our neighbour,
  God's will is done;
in our worldwide task of caring
for the hungry and despairing;
in the harvests we are sharing,
  God's will is done.

3 For the harvests of the Spirit,
  thanks be to God!
For the good we all inherit,
  thanks be to God!
For the wonders that astound us,
for the truths that still confound us;
most of all, that love has found us,
  thanks be to God!

Frederick Pratt Green (b. 1903)

23

1 From heav'n you came, helpless babe,
enter'd our world, your glory veil'd;
not to be served but to serve,
and give your life that we might live.

> *This is our God, the Servant King,*
> *he calls us now to follow him,*
> *to bring our lives as a daily offering*
> *of worship to the Servant King.*

2 There in the garden of tears,
my heavy load he chose to bear;
his heart wth sorrow was torn,
'Yet not my will but yours,' he said.

3 Come see his hands and his feet,
the scars that speak of sacrifice,
hands that flung stars into space
to cruel nails surrendered.

4 So let us learn how to serve,
and in our lives enthrone him;
each other's needs to prefer,
for it is Christ we're serving.

Graham Kendrick (b. 1950)

24

For you are my God;
you alone are my joy.
Defend me, O Lord.

1 You give marvellous comrades to me:
   the faithful who dwell in your land.
   Those who choose alien gods
   have chosen an alien band.

2 You are my portion and cup;
   it is you that I claim for my prize.
   Your heritage is my delight,
   the lot you have given to me.

3 Glad are my heart and my soul;
   securely my body shall rest.
   For you will not leave me for dead,
   nor lead your beloved astray.

4 You show me the path for my life;
   in your presence the fulness of joy.
   To be at your right hand for ever
   for me would be happiness always.

John B. Foley
based on Psalm 16

25

1 Fruitful trees, the Spirit's sowing,
   may we ripen and increase,
   fruit to life eternal growing,
   rich in love and joy and peace.

2 Laden branches freely bearing
   gifts the Giver loves to bless;
   here is fruit that grows by sharing,
   patience, kindness, gentleness.

3 Rooted deep in Christ our master,
Christ our pattern and our goal,
teach us, as the years fly faster,
goodness, faith and self-control.

4 Fruitful trees, the Spirit's tending,
may we grow till harvests cease;
till we taste, in life unending,
heaven's love and joy and peace.

Timothy Dudley-Smith (b. 1926)
based on Galatians 5: 22–3

26

1 Give me oil in my lamp, keep me burning,
give me oil in my lamp, I pray;
give me oil in my lamp, keep me burning,
keep me burning till the break of day.

Sing hosanna, sing hosanna,
sing hosanna to the King of kings!
Sing hosanna, sing hosanna,
sing hosanna to the King!

2 Give me joy in my heart, keep me praising,
give me joy in my heart, I pray;
give me joy in my heart, keep me praising,
keep me praising till the break of day.

3 Give me peace in my heart, keep me loving,
give me peace in my heart, I pray;
give me peace in my heart, keep me loving,
keep me loving till the break of day.

4 Give me love in my heart, keep me serving,
give me love in my heart, I pray;
give me love in my heart, keep me serving,
keep me serving till the break of day.

Traditional

The first verse may be omitted if desired.

27

1 Give to us eyes
that we may truly see,
flight of a bird,
the shapes in a tree,
curve of a hillside,
colours in a stone,
give to us seeing eyes, O Lord.

2 Give to us ears
that we may truly hear,
music in birdsong,
rippling water clear,
whine of the winter wind,
laughter of a friend,
give to us hearing ears, O Lord.

3 Give to us hands
that we may truly know,
patterns in tree bark,
crispness of the snow,
smooth feel of velvet,
shapes in a shell,
give to us knowing hands, O Lord.

Peggy Blakeley

28

1 God forgave my sin in Jesus' name;
I've been born again in Jesus' name,
and in Jesus' name I come to you
to share his love as he told me to.

> *He said:*
> *Freely, freely you have received,*
> *freely, freely give;*
> *go in my name and because you believe,*
> *others will know that I live.*

2 All power is given in Jesus' name,
in earth and heaven in Jesus' name;
and in Jesus' name I come to you
to share his power as he told me to.

Jimmy and Carol Owens

29

God has spoken to his people, hallelujah!
And his words are words of wisdom, hallelujah!
God has spoken to his people, hallelujah!
And his words are words of wisdom, hallelujah!

1 Open your ears, O Christian people,
 open your ears and hear good news.
 Open your hearts, O royal priesthood,
 God has come to you. (*twice*)

2 They who have ears to hear his message,
 they who have ears, then let them hear.
 They who would learn the way of wisdom,
 let them hear God's word. (*twice*)

3 Israel comes to greet the Saviour,
 Judah is glad to see his day.
 From east and west the peoples travel,
 he will show the way. (*twice*)

Willard Francis Jabusch (b. 1930)

30

1 God is here; as we his people
 meet to offer praise and prayer,
 may we find in fuller measure
 what it is in Christ we share.
 Here, as in the world around us,
 all our varied skills and arts
 wait the coming of his Spirit
 into open minds and hearts.

2 Here are symbols to remind us
 of our lifelong need of grace;
 here are table, font and pulpit,
 here the cross has central place;
 here in honesty of preaching,
 here in silence as in speech,
 here in newness and renewal
 God the Spirit comes to each.

3 Here our children find a welcome
  in the Shepherd's flock and fold,
  here, as bread and wine are taken,
  Christ sustains us, as of old.
  Here the servants of the Servant
  seek in worship to explore
  what it means in daily living
  to believe and to adore.

4 Lord of all, of Church and Kingdom,
  in an age of change and doubt
  keep us faithful to the gospel,
  help us work your purpose out.
  Here, in this day's dedication,
  all we have to give, receive.
  We, who cannot live without you,
  we adore you, we believe.

                    Frederick Pratt Green (b. 1903)

31

1 God is love—his the care,
  tending each, everywhere;
  God is love—all is there!
  Jesus came to show him,
  that we all might know him:

      Sing aloud, loud, loud;
      sing aloud, loud, loud:
      God is good,
      God is truth, God is beauty—praise him!

2 Jesus shared all our pain,
  lived and died, rose again,
  rules our hearts, now as then—
  for he came to save us
  by the truth he gave us:

3 To our Lord praise we sing—
  light and life, friend and king,
  coming down love to bring,
  pattern for our duty,
  showing God in beauty:

                    Percy Dearmer (1867–1936)
                    (omitting former verse 2)

32

1 God of Eve and God of Mary,
God of love and mother-earth,
thank you for the ones who with us
shared their life and gave us birth.

2 As you came to earth in Jesus,
so you come to us today;
you are present in the caring
that prepares us for life's way.

3 Thank you, that the Church, our mother,
gives us bread and fills our cup,
and the comfort of the Spirit
warms our hearts and lifts us up.

4 Thank you for belonging, shelter,
bonds of friendship, ties of blood,
and for those who have no children,
yet are parents under God.

5 God of Eve and God of Mary,
Christ our brother, human Son,
Spirit, caring like a mother,
take our love and make us one!

Frederik Herman Kaan (b. 1929)

33

1 Go forth and tell! O Church of God, awake!
God's saving news to all the nations take:
proclaim Christ Jesus, Saviour, Lord, and King,
that all the world his worthy praise may sing.

2 Go forth and tell! God's love embraces all;
he will in grace respond to all who call:
how shall they call if they have never heard
the gracious invitation of his word?

3 Go forth and tell! Where still the darkness lies
   in wealth or want, the sinner surely dies:
   give us, O Lord, concern of heart and mind,
   a love like yours which cares for humankind.

4 Go forth and tell! The doors are open wide:
   share God's good gifts—let no one be denied;
   live out your life as Christ your Lord shall choose,
   your ransomed powers for his sole glory use.

5 Go forth and tell! O Church of God, arise!
   Go in the strength which Christ your Lord supplies;
   go till all nations his great name adore
   and serve him, Lord and King for evermore.

James Edward Seddon (1915–83)

34

1 Go forth for God; go forth to the world in peace;
   be of good courage, armed with heavenly grace,
   in God's good Spirit daily to increase,
   till in his kingdom we behold his face.

2 Go forth for God; go forth to the world in strength;
   hold fast the good, be urgent for the right,
   render to no one evil; Christ at length
   shall overcome all darkness with his light.

3 Go forth for God; go forth to the world in love;
   strengthen the faint, give courage to the weak,
   help the afflicted; richly from above
   his love supplies the grace and power we seek.

4 Go forth for God; go forth to the world in joy,
   to serve God's people every day and hour,
   and serving Christ, our every gift employ,
   rejoicing in the Holy Spirit's power.

5 Sing praise to him who brought us on our way,
   sing praise to him who bought us with his blood,
   sing praise to him who sanctifies each day,
   sing praise to him who reigns one Lord and God.

John Raphael Peacey (1896–1971) and others

35

Go, tell it on the mountain,
over the hills and ev'rywhere.
Go, tell it on the mountain
that Jesus Christ is born.

1 While shepherds kept their watching
   o'er silent flocks by night,
   behold throughout the heavens
   there shone a holy light.

2 The shepherds feared and trembled
   when lo, above the earth
   rang out the angel chorus
   that hailed the Saviour's birth.

3 Down in a lowly manger
   our humble Christ was born;
   and God sent us salvation
   that blessèd Christmas morn.

North American traditional Spiritual

36

1 Great is thy faithfulness, O God my Father,
   there is no shadow of turning with thee;
   thou changest not, thy compassions they fail not,
   as thou hast been thou for ever wilt be.

   Great is thy faithfulness!
   Great is thy faithfulness!
   Morning by morning new mercies I see;
   all I have needed thy hand hath provided—
   great is thy faithfulness, Lord, unto me!

2 Summer and winter, and spring-time and harvest,
   sun, moon and stars in their courses above,
   join with all nature in manifold witness
   to thy great faithfulness, mercy and love.

3 Pardon for sin and a peace that endureth,
   thine own dear presence to cheer and to guide;
   strength for today and bright hope for tomorrow,
   blessings all mine, with ten thousand beside!

Thomas Obediah Chisholm (1866–1960)

37

1 Have you heard the raindrops drumming on the rooftops?
  Have you heard the raindrops dripping on the ground?
  Have you heard the raindrops splashing in the streams
  and running to the rivers all around?

   There's water, water of life,
   Jesus gives us the water of life:
   There's water, water of life,
   Jesus gives us the water of life.

2 There's a busy workman digging in the desert,
  digging with a spade that flashes in the sun:
  soon there will be water rising in the wellshaft,
  spilling from the bucket as it comes.

3 Nobody can live who hasn't any water,
  when the land is dry then nothing much grows:
  Jesus gives us life if we drink the living water,
  sing it so that everybody knows.

Martin Christian Tinn Strover (b. 1932)

38

1 Here from all nations, all tongues, and all peoples,
  countless the crowd but their voices are one;
  vast is the sight and majestic their singing—
  'God has the victory: he reigns from the throne!'

2 These have come out of the hardest oppression;
  now they may stand in the presence of God,
  serving their Lord day and night in his temple,
  ransomed and cleansed by the Lamb's precious blood.

3 Gone is their thirst and no more shall they hunger,
  God is their shelter, his power at their side:
  sun shall not pain them, no burning will torture;
  Jesus the Lamb is their shepherd and guide.

4 He will go with them to clear living water
  flowing from springs which his mercy supplies:
  gone is their grief, and their trials are over;
  God wipes away every tear from their eyes.

5 Blessing and glory and wisdom and power
  be to the Saviour again and again;
  might and thanksgiving and honour for ever
  be to our God: Alleluia! Amen.

Christopher Martin Idle (b. 1938)
based on Revelation 7

39

1 He is Lord, he is Lord;
  he is risen from the dead, and he is Lord;
  every knee shall bow, every tongue confess
  that Jesus Christ is Lord.

2 He is King, he is King;
  he will draw all nations to him, he is King;
  and the time shall be when the world shall sing
  that Jesus Christ is King.

3 He is love, he is love;
  he has shown us by his life that he is love;
  all his people sing with one voice of joy
  that Jesus Christ is love.

4 He is life, he is life;
  he has died to set us free and he is life;
  and he calls us all to live evermore,
  for Jesus Christ is life.

Anon.

40

1 Holy Spirit, come, confirm us
in the truth that Christ makes known;
we have faith and understanding
through your helping gifts alone.

2 Holy Spirit, come, console us,
come as advocate to plead,
loving Spirit from the Father,
grant in Christ the help we need.

3 Holy Spirit, come, renew us,
come yourself to make us live,
holy through your loving presence,
holy through the gifts you give.

4 Holy Spirit, come, possess us,
you the love of Three in One,
Holy Spirit of the Father,
Holy Spirit of the Son.

William Brian Foley (b. 1919)

41

1 How beautiful the morning and the day;
my heart abounds with music, my lips can only say:
how beautiful the morning and the day.

2 How glorious the morning and the day;
my heart is still and listens, my soul begins to pray
to him who is the glory of the day.

3 How bountiful the blessings that he brings
of peace and joy and rapture that makes my spirit sing:
how bountiful the blessings that he brings.

4 How merciful the workings of his grace,
arousing faith and action my soul would never face
without his matchless mercy and his grace.

5 How barren was my life before he came,
supplying love and healing; I live now to acclaim
the majesty and wonder of his name.

Owen Barker

42

1 How lovely on the mountains are the feet of him
who brings good news, good news,
announcing peace, proclaiming news of happiness:
our God reigns, our God reigns!
    Our God reigns! (4 times)

POPULAR VERSION

2 You watchmen, lift your voices joyfully as one,
shout for your king, your king.
See eye to eye the Lord restoring Zion:
your God reigns, your God reigns!
    Your God reigns! (4 times)

3 Waste places of Jerusalem, break forth with joy,
we are redeemed, redeemed.
The Lord has saved and comforted his people:
your God reigns, your God reigns!

4 Ends of the earth, see the salvation of your God,
Jesus is Lord, is Lord.
Before the nations he has bared his holy arm:
your God reigns, your God reigns!

ORIGINAL VERSION

2 He had no stately form, he had no majesty,
that we should be drawn to him.
He was despised and we took no account of him,
yet now he reigns with the most high.
    Now he reigns (3 times)
    with the most high!

3 It was our sin and guilt that bruised and wounded him,
it was our sin that brought him down.
When we like sheep had gone astray, our shepherd came
and on his shoulders bore our shame.
    On his shoulders (3 times)
    he bore our shame.

4 Meek as a lamb that's led out to the slaughterhouse,
dumb as a sheep before its shearer,
his life ran down upon the ground like pouring rain,
that we might be born again.
    That we might be (3 times)
    born again.

5 Out from the tomb he came with grace and majesty,
   he is alive, he is alive.
   God loves us so, see here his hands, his feet, his side,
   yes, we know he is alive.
      He is alive! (4 times)

6 How lovely on the mountains are the feet of him
   who brings good news, good news,
   announcing peace, proclaiming news of happiness:
   our God reigns, our God reigns!
      Our God reigns! (4 times)

Leonard Smith Jnr.

43

1 I danced in the morning
   when the world was begun,
   and I danced in the moon
   and the stars and the sun,
   and I came down from heaven
   and I danced on the earth;
   at Bethlehem I had my birth.

      Dance then wherever you may be;
      I am the Lord of the Dance, said he,
      and I'll lead you all, wherever you may be,
      and I'll lead you all in the dance, said he.

2 I danced for the scribe
   and the pharisee,
   but they would not dance
   and they wouldn't follow me;
   I danced for the fishermen,
   for James and John;
   they came with me
   and the dance went on.

3 I danced on the Sabbath
   and I cured the lame:
   the holy people
   said it was a shame.
   They whipped and they stripped
   and they hung me high,
   and they left me there
   on a cross to die.

4 I danced on a Friday
   when the sky turned black;
   it's hard to dance
   with the devil on your back.
   They buried my body
   and they thought I'd gone;
   but I am the dance
   and I still go on.

5 They cut me down
   and I leap up high;
   I am the life
   that'll never, never die;
   I'll live in you
   if you'll live in me:
   I am the Lord
   of the Dance, said he.

Sydney Carter (b. 1915)

44

1 I sing a song of the saints of God,
   patient and brave and true,
   who toiled and fought and lived and died
   for the Lord they loved and knew;
   and one was a doctor, and one was a queen,
   and one was a shepherdess on the green:
   they were all of them saints of God; and I mean,
   God helping, to be one too.

2 They loved their Lord so good and dear,
   and his love made them strong;
   and they followed the right, for Jesus' sake,
   the whole of their good lives long;
   and one was a soldier, and one was a priest,
   and one was slain by a fierce wild beast:
   and there's not any reason, no, not the least,
   why I shouldn't be one too.

3 They lived not only in ages past,
   there are hundreds of thousands still;
   the world is bright with the joyous saints
   who love to do Jesus' will;
   you can meet them in school, or in lanes, or at sea,
   in church, or in trains, or in shops, or at tea:
   for the saints of God are just like me,
   and I mean to be one too.

Lesbia Scott (1898–1986)

45

I will enter his gates with thanksgiving in my heart;
I will enter his courts with praise;
I will say this is the day that the Lord has made;
I will rejoice for he has made me glad.

He has made me glad, he has made me glad,
I will rejoice for he has made me glad.
He has made me glad, he has made me glad,
I will rejoice for he has made me glad.

based on Psalm 118: 19, 24

46

Jesu, Jesu,
fill us with your love,
show us how to serve
the neighbours we have from you.

1 Kneels at the feet of his friends,
  silently washes their feet,
  master who acts as a slave to them.

2 Neighbours are rich folk and poor,
  neighbours are black, brown and white,
  neighbours are nearby and far away.

3 These are the ones we should serve,
  these are the ones we should love.
  All these are neighbours to us and you.

4 Loving puts us on our knees,
  serving as though we were slaves,
  this is the way we should live with you.

Tom Colvin (c. 1965) and the people of Ghana

47

1 Led like a lamb to the slaughter,
  in silence and shame,
  there on your back you carried a world
  of violence and pain.
  Bleeding, dying, bleeding, dying.

  You're alive, you're alive, you have risen,
  Alleluia!
  And the power and the glory is given,
  Alleluia,
  Jesus to you.

2 At break of dawn, poor Mary,
  still weeping she came,
  when through her grief she heard your voice
  now speaking her name.
  *Mary! Master! Mary! Master!

3 At the right hand of the Father,
  now seated on high,
  you have begun your eternal reign
  of justice and joy.
  Glory, glory, glory, glory.

Graham Kendrick (b. 1950)

*It is effective if the men sing 'Mary!' and the women reply 'Master!'

48

1 Let every Christian pray,
this day, and every day,
come, Holy Spirit, come.
Was not the Church we love
commissioned from above?
Come, Holy Spirit, come.

2 The Spirit brought to birth
the Church of Christ on earth
to seek and save the lost:
never has he withdrawn,
since that tremendous dawn,
his gifts at Pentecost.

3 Age after age, he strove
to teach her how to love:
come, Holy Spirit, come;
age after age, anew
she proved the gospel true:
come, Holy Spirit, come.

4 Only the Spirit's power
can fit us for this hour:
come, Holy Spirit, come;
instruct, inspire, unite;
and make us see the light:
come, Holy Spirit, come.

Frederick Pratt Green (b. 1903)

49

Let there be love shared among us,
let there be love in our eyes,
may now your love sweep this nation,
cause us O Lord to arise,
give us a fresh understanding
of brotherly love that is real,
let there be love shared among us,
let there be love.

Dave Bilbrough

50

1 Long ago, prophets knew
Christ would come, born a Jew,
come to make all things new,
bear his people's burden,
freely love and pardon.

    Ring, bells, ring, ring, ring!
    Sing, choirs, sing, sing, sing!
    When he comes,
    when he comes,
    who will make him welcome?

2 God in time, God in man,
this is God's timeless plan:
he will come, as a man,
born himself of woman,
God divinely human:

3 Mary hail! Though afraid,
she believed, she obeyed.
In her womb God is laid,
till the time expected,
nurtured and protected:

4 Journey ends: where afar
   Bethlem shines, like a star,
   stable door stands ajar.
   Unborn Son of Mary,
   Saviour, do not tarry.

   Ring bells, ring, ring, ring!
   Sing, choirs, sing, sing, sing!
   Jesus comes,
   Jesus comes:
   we will make him welcome.

   Frederick Pratt Green (b. 1903)

51

1 Lord, for the years your love has kept and guided,
   urged and inspired us, cheered us on our way;
   sought us and saved us, pardoned and provided,
   Lord of the years, we bring our thanks today.

2 Lord, for that word, the word of life which fires us,
   speaks to our hearts and sets our souls ablaze;
   teaches and trains, rebukes us and inspires us,
   Lord of the word, receive your people's praise.

3 Lord, for our land, in this our generation,
   spirits oppressed by pleasure, wealth and care;
   for young and old, for this and every nation,
   Lord of our land, be pleased to hear our prayer.

4 Lord, for our world, when we disown and doubt him,
   loveless in strength, and comfortless in pain;
   hungry and helpless, lost indeed without him,
   Lord of the world, we pray that Christ may reign.

5 Lord, for ourselves; in living power remake us—
   self on the cross and Christ upon the throne—
   past put behind us, for the future take us,
   Lord of our lives, to live for Christ alone.

   Timothy Dudley-Smith (b. 1926)

52

Lord Jesus, we enthrone you,
we proclaim you our King.
Standing here in the midst of us
we raise you up with our praise,
and as we worship build a throne,
and as we worship build a throne,
and as we worship build a throne,
come Lord Jesus and take your place.

Paul Gilbert Kyle (b. 1953)
based on Psalm 22: 3

53

1 Lord of all hopefulness, Lord of all joy,
  whose trust, ever childlike, no cares could destroy,
  be there at our waking, and give us, we pray,
  your bliss in our hearts, Lord, at the break of the day.

2 Lord of all eagerness, Lord of all faith,
  whose strong hands were skilled at the plane and the lathe,
  be there at our labours, and give us, we pray,
  your strength in our hearts, Lord, at the noon of the day.

3 Lord of all kindliness, Lord of all grace,
  your hands swift to welcome, your arms to embrace,
  be there at our homing, and give us, we pray,
  your love in our hearts, Lord, at the eve of the day.

4 Lord of all gentleness, Lord of all calm,
  whose voice is contentment, whose presence is balm,
  be there at our sleeping, and give us, we pray,
  your peace in our hearts, Lord, at the end of the day.

Jan Struther (Joyce Placzek) (1901–53)

54

1 Lord of the home, your only Son
received a mother's tender love,
and from an earthly father won
his vision of your home above.

2 Help us, O Lord, our homes to make
your Holy Spirit's dwelling place;
our hands' and hearts' devotion take
to be the servants of your grace.

3 Teach us to keep our homes so fair
that, were our Lord a child once more,
he might be glad our hearth to share,
and find a welcome at our door.

4 Lord, may your Spirit sanctify
each household duty we fulfil;
may we our Master glorify
in glad obedience to your will.

Albert Frederick Bayly (1901–84)

55

1 Lord, you were rich beyond all splendour,
yet, for love's sake, became so poor;
leaving your throne in glad surrender,
sapphire-paved courts for stable floor:
Lord, you were rich beyond all splendour,
yet, for love's sake, became so poor.

2 You are our God beyond all praising,
yet, for love's sake, became a man
stooping so low, but sinners raising
heavenwards, by your eternal plan:
you are our God, beyond all praising,
yet, for love's sake, became a man.

3 Lord, you are love beyond all telling,
Saviour and King, we worship you;
Emmanuel, within us dwelling,
make us and keep us pure and true:
Lord, you are love beyond all telling,
Saviour and King, we worship you.

Frank Houghton (1894–1972)
and in this version Jubilate Hymns

56

1 Lord, the light of your love is shining
in the midst of the darkness, shining;
Jesus, Light of the world, shine upon us,
set us free by the truth you now bring us,
shine on me, shine on me.

Shine, Jesus, shine,
fill this land with the Father's glory;
blaze, Spirit, blaze,
set our hearts on fire.
Flow, river, flow,
flood the nations with grace and mercy;
send forth your word, Lord,
and let there be light.

2 Lord, I come to your awesome presence,
from the shadows into your radiance;
by the blood I may enter your brightness,
search me, try me, consume all my darkness.
Shine on me, shine on me.

3 As we gaze on your kingly brightness,
so our faces display your likeness,
ever changing from glory to glory,
mirrored here may our lives tell your story.
Shine on me, shine on me.

Graham Kendrick (b. 1950)
based on John 1: 1–5; 3: 19–21;
2 Corinthians 3: 18; 1 John 1: 7

57

1 Make me a channel of your peace:
where there is hatred let me bring your love,
where there is injury, your pardon, Lord,
and where there's doubt, true faith in you:
O Master, grant that I may never seek
so much to be consoled as to console;
to be understood as to understand,
to be loved, as to love with all my soul!

2 Make me a channel of your peace:
  where there's despair in life let me bring hope,
  where there is darkness, only light,
  and where there's sadness, ever joy:
      O Master, grant . . .

3 Make me a channel of your peace:
  it is in pardoning that we are pardoned,
  in giving of ourselves that we receive,
  and in dying that we're born to eternal life.

Sebastian Temple
based on the Prayer of St Francis

58

1 Meekness and majesty,
  manhood and deity,
  in perfect harmony,
  the man who is God.
  Lord of eternity
  dwells in humanity,
  kneels in humility
  and washes our feet.

  Oh, what a mystery,
  meekness and majesty,
  bow down and worship,
  for this is your God.

2 Father's pure radiance,
  perfect in innocence,
  yet learns obedience
  to death on a cross.
  Suffering to give us life,
  conquering through sacrifice;
  and as they crucify
  prays 'Father, forgive.'

3 Wisdom unsearchable,
  God the invisible;
  love indestructible
  in frailty appears.
  Lord of infinity
  stooping so tenderly
  lifts our humanity
  to the heights of his throne.

Graham Kendrick (b. 1950)
based on John 3: 13–16,
Philippians 2: 6–11

59

1 Morning has broken
like the first morning;
blackbird has spoken
like the first bird.
Praise for the singing!
Praise for the morning!
Praise for them, springing
fresh from the Word!

2 Sweet the rain's new fall
sunlit from heaven,
like the first dewfall
on the first grass.
Praise for the sweetness
of the wet garden,
sprung in completeness
where his feet pass.

3 Mine is the sunlight!
Mine is the morning
born of the one light
Eden saw play!
Praise with elation,
praise every morning,
God's re-creation
of the new day!

Eleanor Farjeon (1881–1965)

60

1 May the mind of Christ my Saviour
live in me from day to day,
by his love and power controlling
all I do and say.

2 May the word of God enrich me
with his truth from hour to hour,
so that all may see I triumph
only through his power.

3 May the peace of God my Father
in my life for ever reign,
that I may be calm to comfort
those in grief and pain.

4 May the love of Jesus fill me
as the waters fill the sea,
him exalting, self abasing—
this is victory!

5 May his beauty rest upon me
  as I seek to make him known;
  so that all may look to Jesus,
  seeing him alone.

6 May I run the race before me
  strong and brave to face the foe,
  looking only unto Jesus
  as I onward go.

Katie Barclay Wilkinson (1859–1928), altd.

61

1 Not for tongues of heaven's angels,
  not for wisdom to discern,
  not for faith that masters mountains,
  for this better gift we yearn:
  May love be ours, O Lord.

2 Love is humble, love is gentle,
  love is tender, true and kind;
  love is gracious, ever-patient,
  generous of heart and mind:
  May love be ours, O Lord.

3 Never jealous, never selfish,
  love will not rejoice in wrong;
  never boastful nor resentful,
  love believes and suffers long:
  May love be ours, O Lord.

4 In the day this world is fading
  faith and hope will play their part;
  but when Christ is seen in glory
  love shall reign in every heart:
  May love be ours, O Lord.

Timothy Dudley-Smith (b. 1926)
based on 1 Corinthians 13

62

1 O Breath of life, come sweeping through us,
  revive your Church with life and power.
  O Breath of life, come, cleanse, renew us,
  and fit your Church to meet this hour.

2 O Wind of God, come, bend us, break us,
  till humbly we confess our need;
  then in your tenderness re-make us,
  revive, restore, for this we plead.

3 O Breath of love, come breathe within us,
  renewing thought and will and heart;
  come, love of Christ, afresh to win us,
  revive your Church in every part.

4 Revive us, Lord! Is zeal abating
  while harvest fields are vast and white?
  Revive us, Lord, the world is waiting,
  equip your Church to spread the light.

Elizabeth (Bessie) Ann Porter Head (1850–1936)

63

1 O Christ, the healer, we have come
  to pray for health, to plead for friends.
  How can we fail to be restored
  when reached by love that never ends?

2 From every ailment flesh endures
  our bodies clamour to be freed;
  yet in our hearts we would confess
  that wholeness is our deepest need.

3 In conflicts that destroy our health
  we recognize the world's disease;
  our common life declares our ills.
  Is there no cure, O Christ, for these?

4 Grant that we all, made one in faith,
  in your community may find
  the wholeness that, enriching us,
  shall reach and prosper humankind.

Frederick Pratt Green (b. 1903)

64

1 O Christ the same, through all our story's pages,
  our loves and hopes, our failures and our fears;
  eternal Lord, the King of all the ages,
  unchanging still, amid the passing years—
  O living Word, the source of all creation,
  who spread the skies, and set the stars ablaze,
  O Christ the same, who wrought our whole salvation,
  we bring our thanks to you for all our yesterdays.

2 O Christ the same, the friend of sinners sharing
   our inmost thoughts, the secrets none can hide,
   still as of old upon your body bearing
   the marks of love, in triumph glorified—
   O Son of Man, who stooped for us from heaven,
   O Prince of life, in all your saving power,
   O Christ the same, to whom our hearts are given,
   we bring our thanks to you for this the present hour.

3 O Christ the same, secure within whose keeping
   our lives and loves, our days and years remain,
   our work and rest, our waking and our sleeping,
   our calm and storm, our pleasure and our pain—
   O Lord of love, for all our joys and sorrows,
   for all our hopes, when earth shall fade and flee,
   O Christ the same, beyond our brief tomorrows,
   we bring our thanks to you for all that is to be.

Timothy Dudley-Smith (b. 1926)
based on Hebrews 13: 8

65

O let us spread the pollen of peace
throughout our land,
let us spread the pollen of peace
throughout our land.
Let us spread the pollen of peace,
and make all hatred cease;
let us spread the pollen of peace
throughout our land.

1 Oh Christ has sown the seeds of love;
  Christ has launched the wingèd dove.
  Let us make the flower grow
  and let the people know
  that Christ has sown the seeds of love.

2 All it needs is our love to make it grow;
  all it needs is our hopefulness to show,
  and tell those who are choked with fear
  that the Prince of Peace is here;
  all it needs is our love to make it grow.

Roger Brian Courtney (b. 1954)
written for the Corrymeela Community

66

1 O Lord my God! When I in awesome wonder
   consider all the works thy hand hath made,
   I see the stars, I hear the mighty thunder,
   thy pow'r throughout the universe display'd:

   Then sings my soul, my Saviour God, to thee,
   How great thou art! How great thou art!
   Then sings my soul, my Saviour God, to thee,
   How great thou art! How great thou art!

2 When through the woods and forest glades I wander,
   and hear the birds sing sweetly in the trees;
   when I look down from lofty mountain grandeur,
   and hear the brook, and feel the gentle breeze:

3 And when I think that God his Son not sparing,
   sent him to die—I scarce can take it in.
   That on the cross my burden gladly bearing,
   he bled and died to take away my sin:

4 When Christ shall come with shout of acclamation
   and take me home—what joy shall fill my heart!
   Then I shall bow in humble adoration
   and there proclaim, my God, how great thou art!

Russian hymn, tr. Stuart K. Hine (b. 1899)
based on Psalm 8; Romans 5: 9–11;
1 Thessalonians 4: 16–17

67

1 O Lord of creation, to you be all praise!
   Most mighty your working, most wondrous your ways!
   Your glory and might are beyond us to tell,
   and yet in the heart of the humble you dwell.

2 O Lord of all power, I give you my will,
   in joyful obedience your tasks to fulfil.
   Your bondage is freedom; your service is song;
   and, held in your keeping, my weakness is strong.

3 O Lord of all wisdom, I give you my mind,
   rich truth that surpasses our knowledge to find;
   what eye has not seen and what ear has not heard
   is taught by your Spirit and shines from your Word.

4 O Lord of all bounty, I give you my heart;
   I praise and adore you for all you impart,
   your love to inspire me, your counsel to guide,
   your presence to shield me, whatever betide.

5 O Lord of all being, I give you my all;
   if I ever disown you, I stumble and fall;
   but, led in your service your word to obey,
   I'll walk in your freedom to the end of the way.

Jack Copley Winslow (1882–1974), altd.

68

1 O Lord of every shining constellation
   that wheels in splendour through the midnight sky:
   grant us your Spirit's true illumination
   to read the secrets of your work on high.

2 You, Lord, have made the atom's hidden forces;
   your laws its mighty energies fulfil:
   teach us, to whom you give such rich resources,
   in all we use, to serve your holy will.

3 O Life, awaking life in cell and tissue;
   from flower to bird, from beast to brain of man:
   help us to trace, from birth to final issue,
   the sure unfolding of your ageless plan.

4 You, Lord, have stamped your image on your creatures
   and, though they mar that image, love them still:
   lift up our eyes to Christ, that in his features
   we may discern the beauty of your will.

5 Great Lord of nature, shaping and renewing,
   you made us more than nature's sons to be;
   you help us tread, with grace our souls enduing,
   the road to life and immortality.

Albert Frederick Bayly (1901–84)

69

1 O sing a song of Bethlehem,
   of shepherds watching there,
   and of the news that came to them
   from angels in the air:
   the light that shone on Bethlehem
   fills all the world today;
   of Jesus' birth and peace on earth
   the angels sing alway.

2 O sing a song of Nazareth,
   of sunny days of joy,
   O sing of fragrant flowers' breath
   and of the sinless boy:
   for now the flowers of Nazareth
   in every heart may grow;
   now spreads the fame of his dear name
   on all the winds that blow.

3 O sing a song of Galilee,
   of lake and woods and hill,
   of him who walked upon the sea
   and bade its waves be still:
   for though, like waves on Galilee,
   dark seas of trouble roll,
   when faith has heard the Master's word,
   falls peace upon the soul.

4 O sing a song of Calvary,
   its glory and dismay;
   of him who hung upon the tree,
   and took our sins away:
   for he who died on Calvary
   is risen from the grave,
   and Christ our Lord, by heaven adored,
   is mighty now to save.

Louis Fitzgerald Benson (1855–1930)

70

1 One more step along the world I go,
   one more step along the world I go:
   from the old things to the new
   keep me travelling along with you:

   And it's from the old I travel to the new;
   keep me travelling along with you.

2 Round the corner of the world I turn,
more and more about the world I learn;
all the new things that I see
you'll be looking at along with me:

3 As I travel through the bad and good,
keep me travelling the way I should;
where I see no way to go
you'll be telling me the way, I know:

4 Give me courage when the world is rough,
keep me loving though the world is tough;
leap and sing in all I do,
keep me travelling along with you:

5 You are older than the world can be,
you are younger than the life in me;
ever old and ever new,
keep me travelling along with you:

Sydney Carter (b. 1915)

71

1 O Lord, the clouds are gathering,
the fire of judgement burns,
how we have fallen!
O Lord, you stand appall'd to see
your laws of love so scorn'd
and lives so broken.

> *Have mercy, Lord,*
> *forgive us, Lord,*
> *restore us, Lord,*
> *revive your Church again.*
> *Let justice flow like rivers*
> *and righteousness like a*
> *never failing stream.*

2 O Lord, over the nations now
where is the dove of peace?
Her wings are broken.
O Lord, while precious children starve
the tools of war increase;
their bread is stolen.

3 O Lord, dark powers are poised to flood
   our streets with hate and fear;
   we must awaken!
   O Lord, let love reclaim the lives
   that sin would sweep away
   and let your kingdom come.

4 Yet, O Lord, your glorious cross shall tower
   triumphant in this land,
   evil confounding.
   Through the fire your suff'ring Church display
   the glories of her Christ:
   praises resounding!

Graham Kendrick (b. 1950)
based on Isaiah 58: 6–9; Amos 5: 24

72

1 Promised Lord and Christ is he,
  May we soon his kingdom see.

   Come, O Lord, quickly come.
   Come in glory,
   come in glory,
   come in glory,
   quickly come.

2 Teaching, healing, once was he.
  May we soon his kingdom see.

3 Dead and buried once was he.
  May we soon his kingdom see.

4 Risen from the dead is he.
  May we soon his kingdom see.

5 Soon to come again is he.
  May we soon his kingdom see.

Roger Ruston

73

1 Rise and hear! The Lord is speaking,
  as the gospel words unfold;
  we, in all our agelong seeking,
  find no firmer truth to hold.

2 Word of goodness, truth, and beauty,
  heard by simple folk and wise,
  word of freedom, word of duty,
  word of life beyond our eyes.

3 Word of God's forgiveness granted
   to the wild or guilty soul,
   word of love that works undaunted,
   changes, heals, and makes us whole.

4 Speak to us, O Lord, believing,
   as we hear, the sower sows;
   may our hearts, your word receiving,
   be the good ground where it grows.

Howard Charles Adie Gaunt (1902–83)

74

Rejoice! Rejoice! Christ is in you,
the hope of glory in our hearts.
He lives! He lives! His breath is in you,
arise a mighty army, we arise.

1 Now is the time for us
   to march upon the land,
   into our hands
   he will give the ground we claim.
   He rides in majesty
   to lead us into victory,
   the world shall see
   that Christ is Lord!

2 God is at work in us
   his purpose to perform,
   building a kingdom
   of power not of words,
   where things impossible
   by faith shall be made possible;
   let's give the glory
   to him now.

3 Though we are weak, his grace
   is everything we need;
   we're made of clay
   but this treasure is within.
   He turns our weaknesses
   into his opportunities,
   so that the glory
   goes to him.

Graham Kendrick (b. 1950)
based on 1 Corinthians 4: 20;
2 Corinthians 4: 7; 12: 10; Colossians 1: 27

75

1   Safe in the shadow of the Lord
    beneath his hand and power,
    I trust in him,
    I trust in him,
    my fortress and my tower.

2   My hope is set on God alone
    though Satan spreads his snare,
    I trust in him,
    I trust in him,
    to keep me in his care.

3   From fears and phantoms of the night,
    from foes about my way,
    I trust in him,
    I trust in him,
    by darkness as by day.

4   His holy angels keep my feet
    secure from every stone;
    I trust in him,
    I trust in him,
    and unafraid go on.

5   Strong in the Everlasting Name,
    and in my Father's care,
    I trust in him,
    I trust in him,
    who hears and answers prayer.

6   Safe in the shadow of the Lord,
    possessed by love divine,
    I trust in him,
    I trust in him,
    and meet his love with mine.

Timothy Dudley-Smith (b. 1926)
based on Psalm 91

76

Seek, O seek the Lord, while he is near;
trust him, speak to him in prayer,
and he will hear.

1 God be with us in our lives,
   direct us in our calling;
   break the snares the world contrives,
   keep us from falling.

2 God, increase in us the life
   that Christ by dying gave us:
   though we faint in mortal strife
   his blood will save us.

3 Strengthen in our hearts the love
   we owe to one another;
   how can we love God above
   and not our brother?

James Phillip McAuley (1917–76)
based on Isaiah 55

77

1 Seek ye first the kingdom of God,
   and his righteousness,
   and all these things shall be added unto you;
   Allelu-, alleluia:

   Alleluia, alleluia, alleluia, alleluia!

2 Ask, and it shall be given unto you;
   seek, and ye shall find;
   knock, and the door shall be opened unto you;
   Allelu-, alleluia:

3 Man shall not live by bread alone,
   but by every word
   that proceeds from the mouth of the Lord;
   Allelu-, alleluia:

Karen Lafferty
based on Matthew 6: 33 and 7: 7,
and Deuteronomy 8: 3

78

1 'Set your troubled hearts at rest'—
   hear again the word divine;
   all our Father does is best;
   let his peace be yours and mine.

2 Trusting still in God above,
   set your troubled hearts at rest;
   find within a Father's love
   comfort for a soul distressed.

3 When you come to make request
   know that God will answer prayer;
   set your troubled hearts at rest,
   safe within a Father's care.

4 Be at peace, then, and rejoice,
   loved and comforted and blessed;
   hear again the Saviour's voice:
   'Set your troubled hearts at rest.'

Timothy Dudley-Smith (b. 1926)
based on John 14: 1

79

Spirit of God, unseen as the wind,
gentle as is the dove;
teach us the truth and help us believe,
show us the Saviour's love.

1 You spoke to us long, long ago,
   gave us the written word;
   we read it still, needing its truth,
   through it God's voice is heard.

2 Without your help we fail our Lord,
   we cannot live his way;
   we need your power, we need your strength,
   following Christ each day.

Margaret Old (b. 1932)

80

1 Thanks to God whose Word was spoken
in the deed that made the earth.
His the voice that called a nation,
his the fires that tried her worth.
God has spoken:
praise him for his open Word.

2 Thanks to God whose Word incarnate
glorified the flesh of man.
Deeds and words and death and rising
tell the grace in heaven's plan.
God has spoken:
praise him for his open Word.

3 Thanks to God whose Word was written
in the Bible's sacred page,
record of the revelation
showing God to every age.
God has spoken:
praise him for his open Word.

4 Thanks to God whose Word is published
in the tongues of every race.
See its glory undiminished
by the change of time or place.
God has spoken:
praise him for his open Word.

5 Thanks to God whose Word is answered
by the Spirit's voice within.
Here we drink of joy unmeasured,
life redeemed from death and sin.
God is speaking:
praise him for his open Word.

Reginald Thomas Brooks (1918–85)

81

1 The King is among us,
his Spirit is here;
let's draw near and worship,
let songs fill the air.

2 He looks down upon us,
delight in his face,
enjoying his children's love,
enthralled by our praise.

3 For each child is special,
   accepted and loved,
   a love gift from Jesus
   to his Father above.

4 And now he is giving
   his gifts to us all,
   for no one is worthless
   and each one is called.

5 The Spirit's anointing
   on all flesh comes down,
   and we shall be channels
   for works like his own.

6 We come now believing
   your promise of power,
   for we are your people
   and this is your hour.

7 The King is among us,
   his Spirit is here;
   let's draw near and worship,
   let songs fill the air.

Graham Kendrick (b. 1950)

82

The light of Christ has come into the world;
the light of Christ has come.

1 We must all be born again to see the kingdom of God;
the water and the Spirit bring new life in God's love.

2 God gave up his only Son out of love for the world,
so that all who believe in him will live for ever.

3 The light of Christ has come to us so that we might have salvation;
from the darkness of our sins we walk into glory with Christ Jesus.

Donald Fishel (b. 1928)
based on John 3

83

1 The sinless one to Jordan came
to share our fallen nature's blame;
God's righteousness he thus fulfilled
and chose the path his Father willed.

2 Uprising from the waters there,
the voice from heaven did witness bear
that he, the Son of God, had come
to lead his scattered people home.

3 Above him see the heavenly Dove,
the sign of God the Father's love,
now by the Holy Spirit shed
upon the Son's anointed head.

4 How blest that mission then begun
to heal and save a race undone;
straight to the wilderness he goes
to wrestle with his people's foes.

5 Dear Lord, let those baptized from sin
go forth with you, a world to win;
and send the Holy Spirit's power
to shield them in temptation's hour.

6 On you shall all your people feed
and know you are the Bread indeed,
who gives eternal life to those
that with you died, and with you rose.

George Boorne Timms (b. 1910)

84

1 The Spirit came, as promised,
in God's appointed hour;
and now to each believer
he comes in love and power:
and by his Holy Spirit
God seals us as his own,
and through his Son and Spirit
makes access to his throne.

2 The Spirit makes our bodies
the temple of the Lord;
he binds us all together
in faith and true accord:
the Spirit in his greatness
brings power from God above
and with the Son and Father
dwells in our hearts in love.

3 He bids us live together
   in unity and peace,
   employ his gifts in blessing
   and let base passions cease:
   we should not grieve the Spirit
   by open sin or shame,
   nor let our words and actions
   deny his holy name.

4 The word, the Spirit's weapon,
   will bring all sin to light;
   and prayer, by his directing,
   will add new joy and might:
   be filled then with his Spirit,
   live out God's will and word;
   rejoice with hymns and singing,
   make music to the Lord!

James Edward Seddon (1915–83)

85

1 The voice of God goes out to all the world;
   his glory speaks across the universe.
   The great King's herald cries from star to star:
   with power, with justice, he will walk his way.

2 The Lord has said: 'Receive my messenger,
   my promise to the world, my pledge made flesh,
   a lamp to every nation, light from light':
   with power, with justice, he will walk his way.

3 The broken reed he will not trample down,
   nor set his heel upon the dying flame.
   He binds the wounds, and health is in his hand:
   with power, with justice, he will walk his way.

4 Anointed with the Spirit and with power,
   he comes to crown with comfort all the weak,
   to show the face of justice to the poor:
   with power, with justice, he will walk his way.

5 His touch will bless the eyes that darkness held,
   the lame shall run, the halting tongue shall sing,
   and prisoners laugh in light and liberty:
   with power, with justice, he will walk his way.

Peter Icarus

86

1 There is a Redeemer,
Jesus, God's own Son,
precious Lamb of God, Messiah,
Holy One.

Thank you, O my Father,
for giving us your Son,
and leaving your Spirit
till the work on earth is done.

2 Jesus my Redeemer,
Name above all names,
precious Lamb of God, Messiah,
O for sinners slain.

3 When I stand in glory
I will see his face,
and there I'll serve my King for ever,
in that holy place.

Melody Green
based on Isaiah 47: 4; Acts 1: 8;
Philippians 2: 9; Revelation 22: 3–4

87

1 There is singing in the desert, there is laughter in the skies,
there are wise men filled with wonder, there are shepherds with surprise,
you can tell the world is dancing by the light that's in their eyes,
for Jesus Christ is here.

Come and sing aloud your praises,
come and sing aloud your praises,
come and sing aloud your praises,
for Jesus Christ is here.

2 He hears deaf men by the lakeside, he sees blind men in the streets,
he goes up to those who cannot walk, he talks to all he meets,
touching silken robes or tattered clothes, it's everyone he greets,
for Jesus Christ is here.

Geoffrey Marshall-Taylor (b. 1943)

88

1 There's a spirit in the air,
   telling Christians everywhere:
   'Praise the love that Christ revealed,
   living, working, in our world.'

2 Lose your shyness, find your tongue,
   tell the world what God has done:
   God in Christ has come to stay.
   Live tomorrow's life today!

3 When believers break the bread,
   when a hungry child is fed,
   praise the love that Christ revealed,
   living, working, in our world.

4 Still his Spirit gives us light,
   seeing wrong and setting right:
   God in Christ has come to stay.
   Live tomorrow's life today!

5 When a stranger's not alone,
   where the homeless find a home,
   praise the love that Christ revealed,
   living, working, in our world.

6 May the Spirit fill our praise,
   guide our thoughts and change our ways.
   God in Christ has come to stay.
   Live tomorrow's life today!

7 There's a Spirit in the air,
   calling people everywhere:
   praise the love that Christ revealed,
   living, working, in our world.

Brian Arthur Wren (b. 1936)

89

1 Thine be the glory, risen, conquering Son,
   endless is the victory thou o'er death hast won;
   angels in bright raiment rolled the stone away,
   kept the folded grave-clothes where thy body lay:

   Thine be the glory, risen, conquering Son,
   endless is the victory thou o'er death hast won.

2 Lo, Jesus meets us, risen from the tomb;
   lovingly he greets us, scatters fear and gloom;
   let the Church with gladness hymns of triumph sing,
   for her Lord now liveth, death hath lost its sting:

3 No more we doubt thee, glorious Prince of Life;
   life is nought without thee: aid us in our strife;
   make us more than conquerors through thy deathless love;
   bring us safe through Jordan to thy home above:

Edmond Louis Budry (1854–1932)
tr. Richard Birch Hoyle (1875–1939)

90

1 'This is my will,
   my one command,
   that love should dwell
   among you all.
   This is my will,
   that you should love
   as I have shown
   that I love you.

2 No greater love
   can be than this:
   to choose to die
   to save one's friends.
   You are my friends
   if you obey
   what I command
   that you should do.

3 I call you now
   no longer slaves;
   no slave knows all
   his master does.
   I call you friends,
   for all I hear
   my Father say
   you hear from me.

4 You chose not me,
   but I chose you,
   that you should go
   and bear much fruit.
   I chose you out
   that you in me
   should bear much fruit
   that will abide.

5 All that you ask
   my Father dear
   for my name's sake
   you shall receive.
   This is my will,
   my one command,
   that love should dwell
   in each, in all.'

James Quinn (b. 1919)
based on John 15: 12–17

91

1 This is the day that the Lord has made.
   We will rejoice and be glad in it.

2 This is the day when he rose again.
   We will rejoice and be glad in it.

3 This is the day when the Spirit came.
   We will rejoice and be glad in it.

based on Psalm 118: 24

92

1 To God be the glory! Great things he hath done!
   So loved he the world that he gave us his Son;
   who yielded his life an atonement for sin,
   and opened the life gate that all may go in.

   Praise the Lord! Praise the Lord! Let the earth hear his voice!
   Praise the Lord! Praise the Lord! Let the people rejoice!
   O come to the Father, through Jesus the Son:
   and give him the glory! Great things he hath done!

2 O perfect redemption, the purchase of blood!
   To every believer the promise of God;
   the vilest offender who truly believes,
   that moment from Jesus a pardon receives.

3 Great things he hath taught us, great things he hath done,
   and great our rejoicing through Jesus the Son;
   but purer, and higher, and greater will be
   our wonder, our rapture, when Jesus we see.

Frances van Alstyne (1820–1915)

93

1 We have a gospel to proclaim,
good news for all throughout the earth;
the gospel of a Saviour's name:
we sing his glory, tell his worth.

2 Tell of his birth at Bethlehem,
not in a royal house or hall
but in a stable dark and dim:
the Word made flesh, a light for all.

3 Tell of his death at Calvary,
hated by those he came to save;
in lonely suffering on the cross
for all he loved, his life he gave.

4 Tell of that glorious Easter morn:
empty the tomb, for he was free;
he broke the power of death and hell
that we might share his victory.

5 Tell of his reign at God's right hand,
by all creation glorified;
he sends his Spirit on his Church
to live for him, the Lamb who died.

6 Now we rejoice to name him King;
Jesus is Lord of all the earth:
this gospel-message we proclaim,
we sing his glory, tell his worth.

Edward Joseph Burns (b. 1938)

94

1 We turn to Christ anew
who hear his call today,
his way to walk, his will pursue,
his word obey.
To serve him as our king
and of his kingdom learn,
from sin and every evil thing
to him we turn.

2 We trust in Christ to save;
  in him new life begins:
  who by his cross a ransom gave
  for all our sins.
  Our spirits' strength and stay
  who when all flesh is dust
  will keep us in that final day,
  in him we trust.

3 We would be true to him
  till earthly journeys end,
  whose love no passing years can dim,
  our changeless friend.
  May we who bear his Name
  our faith and love renew,
  to follow Christ our single aim,
  and find him true.

Timothy Dudley-Smith (b. 1926)

95

1 When God the Spirit came
  upon his Church outpoured
  in sound of wind and sign of flame
  they spread his truth abroad,
  and filled with the Spirit
  proclaimed that Christ is Lord.

2 What courage, power and grace
  that youthful Church displayed!
  To those of every tribe and race
  they witnessed unafraid,
  and filled with the Spirit
  they broke their bread and prayed.

3 They saw God's word prevail,
  his kingdom still increase,
  no part of all his purpose fail,
  no promised blessing cease,
  and filled with the Spirit
  knew love and joy and peace.

4 Their theme was Christ alone,
  the Lord who lived and died,
  who rose to his eternal throne
  at God the Father's side,
  and filled with the Spirit
  the Church was multiplied.

5 So to this present hour
  our task is still the same,
  in pentecostal love and power
  his gospel to proclaim,
  and filled with the Spirit,
  rejoice in Jesus' name.

Timothy Dudley-Smith (b. 1926)
based on Acts 2

96

1 When Jesus came to Jordan
  to be baptized by John,
  he did not come for pardon,
  but as his Father's Son.
  He came to share repentance
  with all who mourn their sins,
  to speak the vital sentence
  with which good news begins.

2 He came to share temptation,
  our utmost woe and loss;
  for us and our salvation
  to die upon the cross.
  So when the Dove descended
  on him, the Son of Man,
  the hidden years had ended,
  the age of grace began.

3 Come, Holy Spirit, aid us
  to keep the vows we make;
  this very day invade us,
  and every bondage break;
  come, give our lives direction,
  the gift we covet most—
  to share the resurrection
  that leads to Pentecost.

Frederick Pratt Green (b. 1903)

97

1 When I needed a neighbour, were you there,
  were you there?
  When I needed a neighbour, were you there?

  *And the creed and the colour and the name
  won't matter,
  were you there?*

2 I was hungry and thirsty, were you there,
  were you there?
  I was hungry and thirsty, were you there?

3 I was cold, I was naked, were you there,
  were you there?
  I was cold, I was naked, were you there?

4 When I needed a shelter, were you there,
  were you there?
  When I needed a shelter, were you there?

5 When I needed a healer, were you there,
  were you there?
  When I needed a healer, were you there?

6 Wherever you travel, I'll be there,
  I'll be there,
  Wherever you travel, I'll be there,

  *And the creed and the colour and the name
  won't matter,
  I'll be there.*

*Sydney Carter (b. 1915)
based on Matthew 25: 31–46*

98

1 Who are we who stand and sing?
We are God's people.
What this bread and wine we bring?
Food for God's people.
As once with twelve Christ spake,
poured wine, and bread did break;
he now of us will make
a faithful people.

2 What command does Christ impart
to us his people?
Soul and strength and mind and heart;
serve me, my people.
As he in love came low,
our world and work to know;
to life he bids us go
to be his people.

3 Who are we who say one creed?
We are God's people.
What the word we hear and read?
Word of God's people.
Through time, in every race,
from earth to farthest space,
we'll be, with Christ's good grace,
a faithful people.

Thomas Herbert O'Driscoll (b. 1928)

99

1 Brother, sister, let me serve you,
let me be as Christ to you.
Pray that I may have the grace
to let you be my servant, too.

2 We are pilgrims on a journey,
and companions on the road;
we are here to help each other
walk the mile and bear the load.

3 I will hold the Christ-light for you
   in the night-time of your fear;
   I will hold my hand out to you,
   speak the peace you long to hear.

4 I will weep when you are weeping;
   when you laugh I'll laugh with you.
   I will share your joy and sorrow
   'til we've seen this journey through.

5 When we sing to God in heaven
   we shall find such harmony,
   born of all we've known together
   of Christ's love and agony.

6 Won't you let me be your servant,
   let me be as Christ to you?
   Pray that I may have the grace
   to let you be my servant, too.

Richard Gillard

100

1 Would you walk by on the other side,
   when someone called for aid?
   Would you walk by on the other side,
   and would you be afraid?

> *Cross over the road, my friend,*
> *ask the Lord his strength to lend,*
> *his compassion has no end,*
> *cross over the road.*

2 Would you walk by on the other side,
   when you saw a loved one stray?
   Would you walk by on the other side,
   or would you watch and pray?

3 Would you walk by on the other side,
   when starving children cried?
   Would you walk by on the other side,
   and would you not provide?

Pamela Verrall
based on Luke 10: 30–7

101

1 Break thou the bread of life,
    dear Lord, to me,
    as thou didst break the loaves
    beside the sea;
    beyond the sacred page
    I seek thee, Lord,
    my spirit longs for thee,
    O living Word.

2 Bless thou the truth, dear Lord,
    to me, to me,
    as thou didst bless the bread
    by Galilee;
    then shall all bondage cease,
    all fetters fall,
    and I shall find my peace,
    my all in all.

Mary Artemisia Lathbury
(1841–1913)

102

1 Christians, lift your hearts and voices,
    let your praises be outpoured;
    come with joy and exultation
    to the table of the Lord;
    come believing, come expectant,
    in obedience to his word.

2 See, presiding at his table,
    Jesus Christ our great high priest;
    where he summons all his people,
    none is greatest, none is least;
    graciously he bids them welcome
    to the eucharistic feast.

3 Lord, we offer in thanksgiving
    life and work for you to bless;
    yet unworthy is the offering,
    marred by pride and carelessness;
    so, Lord, pardon our transgressions,
    plant in us true holiness.

4 On the evening of his passion
Jesus gave the wine and bread,
so that all who love and serve him
shall for evermore be fed.
Taste and see the Lord is gracious,
feed upon the living bread.

John Edward Bowers (b. 1923)

103

1 He gave his life in selfless love,
for sinners once he came;
he had no stain of sin himself,
but bore our guilt and shame:
he took the cup of pain and death,
his blood was freely shed;
we see his body on the cross,
we share the living bread.

2 He did not come to call the good
but sinners to repent;
it was the lame, the deaf, the blind
for whom his life was spent:
to heal the sick, to find the lost—
it was for such he came,
and round his table all may come
to praise his holy name.

3 They heard him call his Father's name—
then 'Finished!' was his cry;
like them we have forsaken him
and left him there to die:
the sins that crucified him then
are sins his blood has cured;
the love that bound him to a cross
our freedom has ensured.

4 His body broken once for us
is glorious now above;
the cup of blessing we receive,
a sharing of his love:
as in his presence we partake,
his dying we proclaim
until the hour of majesty
when Jesus comes again.

Christopher Porteous (b. 1935)
and in this version Jubilate Hymns

104

1 'I am the Bread of Life;
   he who comes to me shall not hunger;
   he who believes in me shall not thirst.
   No one can come to me
   unless the Father draw him.'

   *'And I will raise him up, and I will raise him up,
   and I will raise him up on the last day.'*

2 'The bread that I will give
   is my flesh for the life of the world,
   and he who eats of this bread,
   he shall live for ever,
   he shall live for ever.'

3 'Unless you eat
   of the flesh of the Son of Man,
   and drink of his blood,
   and drink of his blood
   you shall not have life within you.'

4 'I am the Resurrection,
   I am the Life.
   He who believes in me,
   even if he die,
   he shall live for ever.'

5 Yes Lord, we believe
   that you are the Christ,
   the Son of God
   who has come
   into the world.

Suzanne Toolan (b. 1927)
based on John 6

105

1 I come with joy to meet my Lord,
   forgiven, loved, and free,
   in awe and wonder to recall
   his life laid down for me.

2 I come with Christians far and near
  to find, as all are fed
  the new community of love
  in Christ's communion bread.

3 As Christ breaks bread and bids us share,
  each proud division ends.
  The love that made us, makes us one,
  and strangers now are friends.

4 And thus with joy we meet our Lord.
  His presence, always near,
  is in such friendship better known,
  we see and praise him here.

5 Together met, together bound,
  we'll go our different ways,
  and as his people in the world
  we'll live and speak his praise.

Brian Arthur Wren (b. 1936)

106

1 Jesus, our Master, on the night that they came
  to take you to prison, to death and to shame,
  you called to your table the friends that you knew,
  and asked them to do this in remembrance of you.

2 Still through the ages your new friends draw near,
  and know when they do so, that you will be here;
  we know you are present, though just out of view,
  to meet those who gather in remembrance of you.

3 When it is over, and all gone away,
  come back to our thoughts for the rest of the day,
  and stay with us always, who met here to do
  the thing you commanded, in remembrance of you.

Michael Edward Hewlett (b. 1916)

107

1 Jesus, stand among us
at the meeting of our lives,
be our sweet agreement
at the meeting of our eyes;

O Jesus, we love you,
so we gather here,
join our hearts in unity
and take away our fear.

2 So to you we're gathering
out of each and every land,
Christ the love between us
at the joining of our hands;

3 Jesus stand among us
at the breaking of the bread,
join us as one body
as we worship you, our head.

Graham Kendrick (b. 1950)
based on Matthew 18: 20

108

1 Let us break bread together, we are one;
let us break bread together, we are one;

We are one as we stand*
with our face to the risen Son,
O Lord, have mercy on us.

2 Let us drink wine together . . . (*etc.*)

3 Let us praise God together . . . (*etc.*)

American Traditional Folk Hymn

*The word 'kneel' may be substituted
for 'stand' when appropriate.

109

1 Love is his word, love is his way,
feasting with friends, fasting alone,
living and dying, rising again,
love, only love, is his way:

Richer than gold is the love of my Lord,
better than splendour and wealth.

2 Love is his way, love is his mark,
sharing his last Passover feast.
Christ at his table, host to the twelve,
love, only love, is his mark:

3 Love is his mark, love is his sign,
bread for our strength, wine for our joy,
'This is my body, this is my blood'—
love, only love, is his sign:

4 Love is his sign, love is his news,
'Do this,' he said, 'lest you forget
all my deep sorrow, all my dear blood'—
love, only love, is his news:

5 Love is his news, love is his name,
we are his own, chosen and called,
family, brethren, cousins and kin,
love, only love, is his name:

6 Love is his name, love is his law,
hear his command, all who are his:
'Love one another, I have loved you'—
love, only love, is his law.

7 Love is his law, love is his word:
love of the Lord, Father and Word,
love of the Spirit, God ever one,
love, only love, is his word:

Luke Connaughton (1917–79)

110

1 An upper room did our Lord prepare
for those he loved until the end:
and his disciples still gather there,
to celebrate their risen friend.

2 A lasting gift Jesus gave his own—
to share his bread, his loving cup.
Whatever burdens may bow us down,
he by his cross shall lift us up.

3 And after supper he washed their feet,
   for service, too, is sacrament.
   In him our joy shall be made complete—
   sent out to serve, as he was sent.

(Organ introduction)

4 No end there is: we depart in peace.
   He loves beyond our uttermost:
   in every room in our Father's house
   he will be there, as Lord and host.

Frederick Pratt Green (b. 1903)

111

1 At the supper, Christ the Lord
   gathered friends and said the blessing;
   bread was broken, wine was poured,
   faith in Israel's God expressing:
   signs of the forthcoming passion,
   tokens of a great salvation.

2 After supper, Jesus knelt,
   taking towel and bowl of water;
   washing the disciples' feet,
   servant now as well as master:
   'You,' said he, 'have my example—
   let your way of life be humble!'

3 In the fellowship of faith
   Christ himself with us is present;
   supper of the Lord in truth,
   host and master all-sufficient!
   From this table, gladly sharing,
   send us, Lord, to love and caring.

David Mowbray (b. 1938)

112

1 In the quiet consecration
   of this glad communion hour,
   here we rest in you, Lord Jesus,
   taste your love and touch your power.

2 Here we learn through sacred symbol
   all your grace can be and do,
   by this wonderful indwelling—
   you in us, and we in you.

3 Christ the living bread from heaven,
Christ whose blood is drink indeed,
here by faith and with thanksgiving
in our hearts on you we feed.

4 By your death for sin atoning,
by your resurrection-life,
hold us fast in joyful union,
strengthen us to face the strife.

5 While afar in solemn radiance
shines the feast that is to come—
after conflict, heaven's glory,
your great feast of love and home.

Constance Coote (1844–1936)

113

1 Lord Jesus Christ, you have come to us,
you are one with us, Mary's son—
cleansing our souls from all their sin,
pouring your love and goodness in;
Jesus, our love for you we sing, living Lord.

2 Lord Jesus Christ, now and every day
teach us how to pray, Son of God.
You have commanded us to do
this, in remembrance, Lord, of you;
into our lives your power breaks through, living Lord.

3 Lord Jesus Christ, you have come to us,
born as one of us, Mary's son—
led out to die on Calvary,
risen from death to set us free;
living Lord Jesus, help us see you are Lord.

4 Lord Jesus Christ, we would come to you,
live our lives for you, Son of God;
all your commands we know are true;
your many gifts will make us new;
into our lives your power breaks through, living Lord.

Patrick Robert Norman Appleford (b. 1925)

114

1 Put peace into each other's hands
and like a treasure hold it,
protect it like a candle-flame,
with tenderness enfold it.

2 Put peace into each other's hands
with loving expectation;
be gentle in your words and ways
in touch with God's creation.

3 Put peace into each other's hands,
like bread we break for sharing;
look people warmly in the eye:
our life is meant for caring.

4 As at communion, shape your hands
into a waiting cradle;
the gift of Christ receive, revere,
united round the table.

5 Put Christ into each other's hands,
he is love's deepest measure;
in love make peace, give peace a chance
and share it like a treasure.

Frederik Herman Kaan (b. 1929)

115

1 We come as guests invited
when Jesus bids us dine,
his friends on earth united
to share the bread and wine;
the bread of life is broken,
the wine is freely poured,
for us, in solemn token
of Christ our dying Lord.

2 We eat and drink, receiving
from Christ the grace we need,
and in our hearts believing
on him by faith we feed;
with wonder and thanksgiving
for love that knows no end,
we find in Jesus living
our ever-present friend.

3 One bread is ours for sharing,
one single fruitful vine,
our fellowship declaring
renewed in bread and wine—
renewed, sustained and given
by token, sign and word,
the pledge and seal of heaven,
the love of Christ our Lord.

Timothy Dudley-Smith (b. 1926)

116

You satisfy the hungry heart
with gift of finest wheat;
come, give to us, O saving Lord,
the bread of life to eat.

1 As when the shepherd calls his sheep,
   they know and heed his voice;
   so when you call your fam'ly, Lord,
   we follow and rejoice.

2 With joyful lips we sing to you
   our praise and gratitude,
   that you should count us worthy, Lord,
   to share this heav'nly food.

3 Is not the cup we bless and share
   the blood of Christ outpoured?
   Do not one cup, one loaf declare
   our oneness in the Lord?

4 The myst'ry of your presence, Lord,
   no mortal tongue can tell:
   whom all the world cannot contain
   comes in our hearts to dwell.

5 You give yourself to us, O Lord;
   then selfless let us be,
   to serve each other in your name
   in truth and charity.

Omer Westendorf (b. 1916)

117

Alleluia! Alleluia!
Opening our hearts to him,
singing alleluia!
Alleluia! Jesus is our King!

1 Create in us, O God,
   a humble heart that sets us free
   to proclaim the wondrous majesty
   of our Father in heaven.

2 We bear the name of Christ.
   Justified, we meet with him.
   His words and presence calm our fear,
   revealing God, our Father, here.

3 Let kindred voices join,
  honouring the Lamb of God
  who teaches us by bread and wine
  the mystery of his body.

4 Pour out your Spirit on us,
  empowering us to live as one,
  to carry your redeeming love
  to a world enslaved by sin.

Sherrell Prebble and Howard Clark

118

Alleluia, alleluia!

1 As we walk along beside you,
  and we hear you speak of mercy,
  then it seems our hearts are burning
  for we find you in the sharing of the word.

2 As we ask that you stay with us
  and we watch what you are doing,
  then our eyes begin to open
  for we see you in the breaking of the bread.

3 As we reach for you believing
  and we go to love and serve you,
  then our lives will be proclaiming
  that we know you in the rising from the dead.

Lord, alleluia!

Michael Arnold Perry (b. 1942)
based on Luke 24: 13–35

119

1 Father, who in Jesus found us,
  God, whose love is all around us,
  who to freedom new unbound us,
  keep our hearts with joy aflame.

2 For the sacramental breaking,
   for the honour of partaking,
   for your life our lives remaking,
   young and old, we praise your name.

3 From the service of this table
   lead us to a life more stable;
   for our witness make us able;
   blessing on our work we claim.

4 Through our calling closely knitted,
   daily to your praise committed,
   for a life of service fitted,
   let us now your love proclaim.

Frederik Herman Kaan (b. 1929)

120

1 For the bread which you have broken,
   for the wine which you have poured,
   for the words which you have spoken,
   now we give you thanks, O Lord.

2 By these pledges that you love us,
   by your gift of peace restored,
   by your call to heaven above us,
   hallow all our lives, O Lord.

3 In your service, Lord, defend us,
   in our hearts keep watch and ward;
   in the world to which you send us
   let your kingdom come, O Lord.

Louis Fitzgerald Benson (1855–1930)

121

1 Now let us from this table rise
   renewed in body, mind and soul;
   with Christ we die and live again,
   his selfless love has made us whole.

2 With minds alert, upheld by grace,
   to spread the Word in speech and deed,
   we follow in the steps of Christ,
   at one with all in hope and need.

3 To fill each human house with love,
   it is the sacrament of care;
   the work that Christ began to do
   we humbly pledge ourselves to share.

4 Then give us courage, Father God,
   to choose again the pilgrim way,
   and help us to accept with joy
   the challenge of tomorrow's day.

Frederik Herman Kaan (b. 1929)

122

One bread, one body, one Lord of all,
one cup of blessing which we bless;
and we, though many, throughout the earth,
we are one body in this one Lord.

1 Gentile or Jew,
   servant or free,
   woman or man,
   no more.

2 Many the gifts,
   many the works,
   one in the Lord
   of all.

3 Grain for the fields,
   scattered and grown,
   gathered to one,
   for all.

John B. Foley
based on 1 Corinthians 10: 16–17, 12: 4;
Galatians 3: 28; The Didache, 9

123

1 Praise the Lord, rise up rejoicing,
   worship, thanks, devotion voicing:
   glory be to God on high!
   Christ, your cross and passion sharing,
   by this Eucharist declaring
   yours the eternal victory.

2 Scattered flock, one Shepherd sharing,
   lost and lonely, one voice hearing,
   ears are open to your word;
   by your blood new life receiving,
   in your body firm, believing,
   we are yours, and you the Lord.

3 Send us forth alert and living,
sins forgiven, wrongs forgiving,
in your Spirit strong and free.
Finding love in all creation,
bringing peace in every nation,
may we faithful followers be.

Howard Charles Adie Gaunt (1902–83)

124

1 Sent forth by God's blessing, our true faith confessing,
the people of God from his dwelling take leave.
The supper is ended; O now be extended
the fruits of his service in all who believe.
The seed of his teaching, our hungry souls reaching,
shall blossom in action for God and for all.
His grace shall incite us, his love shall unite us
to further God's kingdom and answer his call.

2 With praise and thanksgiving to God who is living,
the tasks of our everyday life we will face.
Our faith ever sharing, in love ever caring,
we claim as our neighbour all those of each race.
One bread that has fed us, one light that has led us
unite us as one in his life that we share.
Then may all the living with praise and thanksgiving
give honour to Christ and his name that we bear.

Omer Westendorf (b. 1916), altd.

125

1 The Lord is here—he finds us as we seek
to learn his will and follow in his way.
He gives himself just as he gave his Word,
the God of promise greets us ev'ry day.

2 The Lord is here—he meets us as we share—
this is the life he calls us now to live;
in offered peace, in shared-out bread and wine,
our God is gift and calls us now to give.

3 The Lord is here—inviting us to go
   and share the news with people everywhere.
   He waits outside in need and help alike,
   the Spirit moves through deed as well as prayer.

4 So let us go, intent to seek and find,
   living this hope that God is always near.
   Sharing and trusting, let us live his love,
   that all the world may say—'The Lord is here.'

Christopher Ellis (b. 1949)

126

1 All created things, bless the Lord;
   all you heavens, bless the Lord;
   all you angels, bless the Lord;
   sing to God and praise his name.

2 Sun and moon and stars of heaven,
   rain and dew and winds that blow,
   fire and heat and ice and snow,
   sing to God and praise his name.

3 Bless the Lord, you nights and days;
   light and darkness, praise him too;
   clouds and lightnings in the sky,
   sing to God and praise his name.

4 Hills and mountains, bless the Lord;
   flowing rivers with the seas,
   flying birds and earthly beasts,
   sing to God and praise his name.

5 All who dwell upon the earth,
   priests and servants of the Lord,
   humble people, holy ones,
   sing to God and praise his name.

6 Bless the Father, bless the Son,
   bless the Spirit, Three in One;
   sound his glory all your days;
   give to God exalted praise.

Edward Flewett Darling (b. 1933)
based on the Benedicite

127

1 Bless the Lord, the God of our fathers:*
   Sing his praise and exalt him for ever.

2 Bless his holy and glorious name:

3 Bless him in his holy and glorious temple:

4 Bless him who beholds the depths:

5 Bless him seated between the cherubim:

6 Bless him on the throne of his kingdom:

7 Bless him in the heights of heav'n:

8 Bless the Father, the Son, and the Holy Spirit:

from the Alternative Prayer Book (1984)

* The word 'forebears' may be substituted for 'fathers'
if desired.

128

1 Blest be the God of Israël,
   the everlasting Lord.
   You come in power to save your own,
   your people Israël.
   For Israël you now raise up
   salvation's tower on high
   in David's house who reigned as king
   and servant of the Lord.

2 Through holy prophets did you speak
   your word in days of old,
   that you would save us from our foes
   and all who bear us ill.
   On Sinaï you gave to us
   your covenant of love;
   so with us now you keep your word
   in love that knows no end.

3 Of old you gave your solemn oath
  to Father Abraham;
  whose seed a mighty race should be
  and blest for evermore.
  You vowed to set your people free
  from fear of every foe,
  that we might serve you all our days
  in goodness, love, and peace.

4 O tiny child, your name shall be
  the prophet of the Lord;
  the way of God you will prepare
  to make God's coming known.
  You shall proclaim to Israël
  salvation's dawning day,
  when God shall wipe away all sin
  with mercy and with love.

5 The rising sun shall shine on us
  to bring the light of day
  to all who sit in darkest night
  and shadow of the grave.
  Our footsteps God shall safely guide
  to walk the ways of peace,
  whose name for evermore be blest,
  who lives and loves and saves.

James Quinn (b. 1919), altd. 1985
based on the Benedictus

129

1 Come, worship God who is worthy of honour,
  enter his presence with thanks and a song!
  He is the rock of his people's salvation,
  to whom our jubilant praises belong.

2 Ruled by his might are the heights of the mountains,
  held in his hands are the depths of the earth;
  his is the sea, his the land, for he made them,
  king above all gods, who gave us our birth.

3 We are his people, the sheep of his pasture,
  he is our maker and to him we pray;
  gladly we kneel in obedience before him—
  great is the God whom we worship this day!

4 Now let us listen, for God speaks among us,
  open our hearts and receive what he says:
  peace be to all who remember his goodness,
  trust in his promises, walk in his ways!

Michael Arnold Perry (b. 1942)
based on Psalm 95; 1–7

130

1 Faithful vigil ended,
  watching, waiting cease:
  Master, grant your servant
  his discharge in peace.

2 All your Spirit promised,
  all the Father willed,
  now these eyes behold it
  perfectly fulfilled.

3 This your great deliverance
  sets your people free;
  Christ their light uplifted
  all the nations see.

4 Christ, your people's glory!
  Watching, doubting cease:
  grant to us your servants
  our discharge in peace.

Timothy Dudley-Smith (b. 1926)
based on the Nunc Dimittis

131

1 Glory and honour and power:
  are yours by right, O Lord our God.

2 For you created all things:
  and by your will they have their being.

3 Glory and honour and power:
  are yours by right, O Lamb for us slain;

4 for by your blood you ransomed men* for God:
  from ev'ry race and language,
  from ev'ry people and nation,

5 to make them* a kingdom of priests:
  to stand and serve before our God.

6 To him who sits on the throne and to the Lamb:
  be praise and honour, glory and might
  for ever and ever. Amen.

from the Alternative Prayer Book (1984)

* The word 'us' may be substituted for 'men'
and 'them' where indicated, if desired.

132

1 Glory in the highest to the God of heaven!
 Peace to all your people through the earth be given:
 mighty God and Father, thanks and praise we bring,
 singing alleluias to our heavenly King.

2 Jesus Christ is risen, God the Father's Son:
 with the Holy Spirit, you are Lord alone!
 Lamb once killed for sinners, all our guilt to bear,
 show us now your mercy, now receive our prayer.

3 Christ the world's true Saviour, high and holy one,
 seated now and reigning from your Father's throne:
 Lord and God, we praise you; highest heaven adores:
 in the Father's glory, all the praise be yours!

Christopher Martin Idle (b. 1938)
based on the Gloria in Excelsis

133

1 God, we praise you! God, we bless you!
 God, we name you sovereign Lord!
 Mighty King whom angels worship,
 Father, by your Church adored:
 all creation shows your glory,
 heaven and earth draw near your throne,
 singing, 'Holy, holy, holy,
 Lord of hosts, and God alone!'

2 True apostles, faithful prophets,
 saints who set their world ablaze,
 martyrs, once unknown, unheeded,
 join one growing song of praise,
 while your Church on earth confesses
 one majestic Trinity:
 Father, Son, and Holy Spirit,
 God, our hope eternally.

3 Jesus Christ, the King of glory,
 everlasting Son of God,
 humble was your virgin mother,
 hard the lonely path you trod:
 by your cross is sin defeated,
 hell confronted face to face,
 heaven opened to believers,
 sinners justified by grace.

4 Christ, at God's right hand victorious,
  you will judge the world you made:
  Lord, in mercy help your servants
  for whose freedom you have paid:
  raise us up from dust to glory,
  guard us from all sin today;
  King enthroned above all praises,
  save your people, God, we pray.

Christopher Martin Idle (b. 1938)
based on the Te Deum

134

Holy, holy, holy Lord,
God of power and might,
Holy, holy, holy Lord,
God of power and might,
heav'n and earth are full of your glory.
Hosanna in the highest.

*Blessed is he who comes in the name of the Lord.
Hosanna in the highest.

Sanctus (International Consultation on English Texts)

* The Benedictus ('Blessed is he') may be omitted if desired.

135

Jubilate, ev'rybody,
serve the Lord in all your ways,
and come before his presence singing:
enter now his courts with praise.
For the Lord our God is gracious,
and his mercy everlasting.
Jubilate, jubilate, jubilate Deo!

from Psalm 100 (the Jubilate)
para. Fred Dunn

136

1 Tell out, my soul, the greatness of the Lord:
unnumbered blessings, give my spirit voice;
tender to me the promise of his word;
in God my Saviour shall my heart rejoice.

2 Tell out, my soul, the greatness of his name:
make known his might, the deeds his arm has done;
his mercy sure, from age to age the same;
his holy name, the Lord, the Mighty One.

3 Tell out, my soul, the greatness of his might:
powers and dominions lay their glory by;
proud hearts and stubborn wills are put to flight,
the hungry fed, the humble lifted high.

4 Tell out, my soul, the glories of his word:
firm is his promise, and his mercy sure.
Tell out, my soul, the greatness of the Lord
to children's children and for evermore.

Timothy Dudley-Smith (b. 1926)
based on the Magnificat

137

1 Living Lord, our praise we render!
His the blood for sinners shed.
In the Father's power and splendour
Christ is risen from the dead.

2 Death's dominion burst and broken
by that Life which no more dies;
we to whom the Lord has spoken,
one with Christ, in freedom rise.

3 One with Christ, both dead and risen;
dead to self and Satan's claim,
raised from death and sin's dark prison,
life is ours through Jesus' name.

Timothy Dudley-Smith (b. 1926)
based on the Easter Anthems

138

Dia do bheath' a naoidhe naoimh,
'sa mhainséar cé taoi bocht
meadhrach saibhir a tá tú
's glórmhar id dhún féin anocht.

1 All hail and welcome, holy child,
you poor babe in the manger.
So happy and rich it is you are
tonight inside your castle.

Dia do bheath' a Íosa 'rís!
'Do bheatha, i gclí on Óigh!
A Ghnuís is áille ná'n ghrian,
na mílte fáilte 'do Dhia óg!

2 God bless you, Jesus, once again!
Your life in its young body,
your face more lovely than the sun—
a thousand welcomes, Baby!

Míle fáilte 'nocht i gclí
le mo chroíse dom Rí fial,
i ndá nádur 'do chuaigh, póg
is fáilte uaim do Dhia!

3 Tonight we greet you in the flesh;
my heart adores my young King.
You came to us in human form—
I bring you a kiss and a greeting.

Aodh Mac Cathmhaoil
(1571–1626)
adpt. Peter Downey (b. 1956)

tr. George Otto Simms
(b. 1910)

139

1 Ag Críost an síol;
ag Críost an fómhar.
In iothlainn Dé
go dtugtar sinn.

1 The seed is Christ's,
and his the sheaf;
within God's barn
may we be stored.

2 Ag Críost an mhuir;
ag Críost an t-iasc.
I líonta Dé
go gcastar sinn.

2 The sea is Christ's;
and his the fish;
in the nets of God
may we be caught.

3 Ó fhás go haois,
is ó aois go bás,
do dhá láimh, a Críost,
anall tharainn.

3 From birth to youth,
and from youth till death,
your two hands, O Christ,
stretch over us.

4 Ó bhás go críoch,
ní críoch ach athfhás,
i bParthas na nGrást
go rabhaimid.

4 From death—the end?
No end—but new life
in sweet Paradise
may we be found.

Anon.

tr. George Otto Simms
(b. 1910)

140

1 Álainn farraige spéirghlas,
  álainn uisceacha ciúin',
  álainn taitneamh na gréine
  ar na tonnta tá fúinn;
  faoileáin 'g eiteal 'sna spéartha,
  teas le héirí an lae;
  Ó! nach álainn an saol!
  Ó! nach álainn, a Dhé!
  Siúd uait amharc na sléibhte
  barr' á bhfolach fá cheo,
  caoirí ciúin' ar a dtaobha,
  síth is sonas is só.

2 Tógfad suas mo chroíse,
  tógfad suas mo ghlór,
  molfad eisean achoíche
  fá gach iontas mór;
  ardaigh feasta mo smaointe
  mar na sléibhte san aer,
  ciúnaigh feasta mo chroíse
  mar an t-uisce soiléir;
  éist lem achainí, a Thiarna,
  tar is cónaigh im chléibh,
  réitigh m'anam; 's im intinn
  déansa t'áras, a Dhé.

Douglas Hyde (An Craoibhín)
(1860–1949)

1 *Beautiful the green-blue sea*
  and the quiet waters,
  beautiful the shining sun
  on the waves below;
  seagulls flying above
  as warmth returns with the day;
  O, how lovely the world is!
  O, how lovely, O God!
  See the hills beyond,
  their summits covered in mist,
  and quiet sheep on their sides,
  O peace, contentment and joy!

2 *I will lift up my heart to God,*
  I will lift up my voice,
  I will praise him evermore
  for his wonderful world;
  like the water clear
  my heart will now be calm,
  like the hills in the air
  my thoughts will now arise,
  hear my prayer, O Lord,
  O come, within me dwell,
  prepare my soul, O God,
  and make your home in my mind.

tr. Anon.
adpt. Donald Davison

*At this point the line order differs from
that in the original.

141

1 Bí, a Íosa, im chroíse i gcuimhne gach uair,
  bí, a Íosa, in chroíse le haithrí go luath,
  bí, a Íosa, im chroíse le cumann go buan,
  ó, a Íosa, 'Dhé dhílis, ná scar thusa uaim.

2 'Sé Íosa mo ríse, mo chara is mo ghrá;
   'sé Íosa mo dhídean ar pheacaí is ar bhás;
   'sé Íosa mo aoibhneas, mo scáthán de ghnáth;
   is a Íosa, 'Dhé dhílis, ná scar uaim go brách.

3 Bí, a Íosa, go síoraí im chroí is im bhéal,
   bí, a Íosa, go síoraí im thuigse mar an gcéann',
   bí, a Íosa, go síoraí im mheabhair mar léann,
   's ó, a Íosa, 'Dhé dhílis, ná fág mé liom féin.

*Anon. (from a manuscript
found in Ulster by Douglas Hyde)*

1 *O Jesus, ev'ry moment be in my heart and mind;*
   O Jesus, stir my heart with sorrow for my sins;
   O Jesus, fill my heart with never-failing love;
   O Jesus, sweet Master, never part from me.

2 *O Jesus is my king, my friend, and my love;*
   O Jesus is my shelter from sinning and from death;
   O Jesus, my gladness, my mirror all my days;
   O Jesus, my dearest Lord, never part from me.

3 *O Jesus, be for ever in my heart and my mouth;*
   O Jesus, be for ever in my thought and my prayer;
   O Jesus, be for ever in my quiet mind;
   O Jesus, my sweet Lord, do not leave me alone.

tr. George Otto Simms (b. 1910)

142

1 All my hope on God is founded;
   he doth still my trust renew,
   me through change and chance he guideth,
   only good and only true,
   God unknown,
   he alone
   calls my heart to be his own.

2 Pride of man and earthly glory,
   sword and crown betray his trust;
   what with care and toil he buildeth,
   tower and temple, fall to dust.
   But God's power,
   hour by hour,
   is my temple and my tower.

3 God's great goodness aye endureth,
   deep his wisdom, passing thought:
   splendour, light, and life attend him,
   beauty springeth out of naught.
   Evermore
   from his store
   new-born worlds rise and adore.

4 Daily doth the almighty giver
   bounteous gifts on us bestow;
   his desire our soul delighteth,
   pleasure leads us where we go.
   Love doth stand
   at his hand;
   joy doth wait on his command.

5 Still from man to God eternal
   sacrifice of praise be done,
   high above all praises praising
   for the gift of Christ his Son.
   Christ doth call
   one and all:
   ye who follow shall not fall.

Joachim Neander (1650–80)
tr. Robert Bridges (1844–1930)

143

1 At the name of Jesus every knee shall bow,
   every tongue confess him King of glory now;
   'tis the Father's pleasure we should call him Lord,
   who from the beginning was the mighty Word.

2 At his voice creation sprang at once to sight,
   all the angel faces, all the hosts of light;
   thrones and dominations, stars upon their way,
   all the heavenly orders, in their great array.

3 Humbled for a season, to receive a name
   from the lips of sinners unto whom he came;
   faithfully he bore it spotless to the last,
   brought it back victorious when from death he passed.

4 Bore it up triumphant with its human light,
   through all ranks of creatures to the central height;
   to the eternal Godhead, to the Father's throne,
   filled it with the glory of his triumph won.

5 Name him, Christians, name him, with love strong as death,
   but with awe and wonder, and with bated breath;
   he is God the Saviour, he is Christ the Lord,
   ever to be worshipped, trusted and adored.

6 In your hearts enthrone him; there let him subdue
all that is not holy, all that is not true;
crown him as your captain in temptation's hour,
let his will enfold you in its light and power.

7 With his Father's glory, Jesus comes again,
angel hosts attend him and announce his reign;
for all wreaths of empire meet upon his brow,
and our hearts confess him King of glory now.

Caroline Maria Noel (1817–77)
and in this version Jubilate Hymns

144

1 O for a thousand tongues to sing
my dear Redeemer's praise,
the glories of my God and King,
the triumphs of his grace!

2 Jesus! The name that charms our fears,
that bids our sorrows cease;
'tis music in the sinner's ears,
'tis life, and health, and peace.

3 He speaks, and, listening to his voice,
new life the dead receive,
the mournful, broken hearts rejoice,
the humble poor believe.

4 Hear him, ye deaf; his praise, ye dumb,
your loosened tongues employ:
ye blind, behold your Saviour come;
and leap, ye lame, for joy.

5 My gracious Master and my God,
assist me to proclaim,
to spread through all the world abroad,
the honours of thy name.

Charles Wesley (1707–88)

145

1 Take my life, and let it be
consecrated, Lord, to thee;
take my moments and my days,
let them flow in ceaseless praise.

2 Take my hands, and let them move
at the impulse of thy love;
take my feet, and let them be
swift and beautiful for thee.

3 Take my voice, and let me sing
always, only, for my King;
take my intellect and use
every power as thou shalt choose.

4 Take my will, and make it thine
it shall be no longer mine;
take my heart, it is thine own;
it shall be thy royal throne.

5 Take my love; my Lord, I pour
at thy feet its treasure store:
take myself, and I will be
ever, only, all, for thee.

Frances Ridley Havergal (1836–7

146

1 What a friend we have in Jesus
all our sins and griefs to bear,
what a privilege to carry
everything to God in prayer;
O what peace we often forfeit,
O what needless pain we bear,
all because we do not carry
everything to God in prayer!

2 Have we trials and temptations,
is there trouble anywhere?
We should never be discouraged:
take it to the Lord in prayer.
Can we find a friend so faithful
who will all our sorrows share?
Jesus knows our every weakness:
take it to the Lord in prayer.

3 Are we weak and heavy-laden,
cumbered with a load of care?
Jesus is our only refuge:
take it to the Lord in prayer.
Do your friends despise, forsake you?
Take it to the Lord in prayer;
in his arms he'll take and shield you,
you will find a solace there.

Joseph Medlicott Scriven (1819–86), altd

ACKNOWLEDGEMENTS

The Hymnal Revision Committee of the Church of Ireland and Oxford University Press
thank the following who have given permission for copyright material to be included. Every
effort has been made to trace copyright owners, and the compilers apologize to anyone
whose rights have inadvertently not been acknowledged. A blank in the third column
indicates that permission has been granted by the author or translator. Particulars of
copyright music will be found in the music edition.

An asterisk indicates a translation.

Author/Translator	Hymn No.	Text used by permission of
Alternative Prayer Book 1984	127, 131	© 1984, the General Synod of the Church of Ireland, published by Collins
Appleford, P.	113	© Josef Weinberger Ltd.
Barker, O.	41	Thankyou Music
Bayly, A. F.	54, 68	Oxford University Press
Bilbrough, D.	49	Thankyou Music
Blakeley, P.	27	A. & C. Black (Publishers) Ltd., from *Someone's Singing, Lord*
Bowers, J. E.	102	
Brooks, R. T.	80	Hope Publishing Company, USA
Burns, E. J.	93	
Carter, S.	43, 70, 97	Stainer & Bell Ltd.
Chisholm, T. O.	36	Hope Publishing Company, USA
Clark, H.	117	Thankyou Music
Coelho, T.	18	Word (UK) Ltd.
Colvin, T.	46	Hope Publishing Company, USA
Connaughton, L.	109	McCrimmon Publishing Co. Ltd.
Courtney, R.	65	
Cross, S.	16	Exors. of Stewart Cross
Darling, E. F.	126	Oxford University Press/© E. F. Darling
Davison, W. D.	140*	Oxford University Press/© W. D. Davison
Downey, P.	138*	
Dudley-Smith, T.	9, 17, 25, 51, 61, 64, 75, 78, 94, 95, 115, 130, 136, 137	
Dunn, F.	135	Thankyou Music
Ellis, C.	125	Oxford University Press
Evans, D.	7	Thankyou Music
Farjeon, E.	59	David Higham Associates
Fishel, D.	1, 82	The Word of God, USA
Foley, J. B.	24, 122	North American Liturgy Resources, USA
Foley, W. B.	40	Faber Music Ltd.
Gaunt, H. C. A.	73, 123	Oxford University Press
Gillard, R.	99	Thankyou Music
Gillman, B.	10	Thankyou Music
Green, F. Pratt	22, 30, 48, 50, 63, 96, 110	Stainer & Bell Ltd.
Green, M.	86	Cherry Lane Music Ltd.
Hewlett, M.	106	Oxford University Press
Hine, S. K.	66*	Thankyou Music
Houghton, F.	55	Overseas Missionary Fellowship/this version Jubilate Hymns
Hyde, D.	140	D. Sealy
Icarus, P.	85	McCrimmon Publishing Co. Ltd.
Idle, C. M.	38, 132, 133	Jubilate Hymns/© C. M. Idle
ICET	134	Copyright © 1970, 1971, 1975, International Consultation on English Texts

INDEX OF FIRST LINES AND TITLES

Where titles differ from first lines they are shown in italic. An asterisk indicates English singing translations of the Irish hymns.